CW00641192

The publishers are grateful to
EXPRESS NEWSPAPERS PLC
without whose generous financial assistance
this book could not have been made.

DR JUNE GOODFIELD has written eleven books, including *An Imagined World, From the Face of the Earth* and *The Planned Miracle* which accompanied a BBC television series of the same name. She is President of International Health and Biomedicine. She is also a Clarence J. Robinson professor at George Mason University in Fairfax, Virginia.

MARY ANNE FITZGERALD is one of the leading journalists on African affairs. She has been covering wars on the African continent for fourteen years as a correspondent for the *Financial Times, Sunday Times* and *Independent*.

Peace in our time?

June Goodfield &
Mary Anne Fitzgerald

C&B
COLLINS & BROWN

First published in Great Britain in 1991
by Collins & Brown Limited
Mercury House
195 Knightsbridge
London SW7 1RE

A CIP catalogue record for this book
is available from the British Library

ISBN 1 85585 091 5

Conceived, edited and designed by Collins & Brown

Managing Editor: Mary Anne Fitzgerald
Editors: Jennifer Chilvers
Colin Ziegler
Art Director: Roger Bristow
Designed by: Sally Smallwood

Filmset by August Filmsetting, St Helens, UK
Reproduction by J. Film, Thailand
Printed and bound in Italy by OFSA s.p.A. Milan

CONTENTS

INTRODUCTION
THE CONSPIRACY OF SILENCE

June Goodfield

There is a dreadful air of permanence attached to war. There was never a time when it did not exist; never a time when it was not brutal; never a time when innocent bystanders, seeking nothing more than the peaceful pursuit of their normal daily lives, were not sucked into the maelstrom of destruction.

Distance tends to glamorize wars. History has smoothed the turmoil into a comprehensible sequence of events leading to geopolitical changes. Every country has its great epics and its own military heroes – Henry V, Charlemagne, Saladin, Alexander the Great, Napoleon and Wellington, Generals Grant and Robert E. Lee. Every country or ethnic grouping remembers and glorifies those moments in their evolution when they conquered or withstood.

The glamour of war still persists. Today's heroes are war photographers such as Don McCullin and James Nachtwey who, against their will, we endow with a macho mystique for being in the thick of the action.

Those such as McCullin and Nachtwey, plus all the others who have contributed to this book, know better. Being witness to the atrocities of war – the Cambodian children who have lost a leg by stepping on a landmine, the Salvadorean peasants who have been beheaded by hit squads, the millions who are homeless, starving, wounded – carves deep into the very soul of mankind.

'Each time you're left with an awareness of something very dark and cruel that you have to carry with you always. The bottom line of war is mutilation and death. If you don't understand that, you don't understand war,' said Nachtwey, who has photographed over fifteen conflicts.

Most of us, however, have become inured to war. Television has given it a sense of immediacy, but not of urgency. Media reports on fighting cannot do justice to a reality which is far more horrific than we could ever imagine. Because it is such a vast problem, impossible for an individual to influence, there is an extraordinary cultural tolerance for armed conflict. The collective outrage demonstrated against the extermination of whales, elephants and rhinos does not exist for the twenty million people who have been killed since the end of World War II.

The profile of war has changed. The military machine that marched through history, albeit often breaking rank, has degenerated into a flailing, amoral behemoth that kills without conscience.

Once the battlefield provided the major focus of devastation. True, as armies swept backwards and forwards across the land, they might rape, loot and burn. Afterwards, flushed with victory or cast down by defeat, they sometimes wreaked a terrible vengeance upon those whose only crime was to be in the wrong place at the wrong time.

The situation was bad for innocent bystanders in past times. Now it is appalling. In some places it is safer these days to be a soldier than an unarmed civilian. In World War I, five per cent of the casualties were civilians. In World War II, it was fifty per cent. In the thirty-two conflicts that were being waged at the end of 1990, ninety per cent of the casualties were civilians. The great majority of these were women and children.

Underpinning these statistics is the growth of internal conflicts. During the post-war period there have been fewer conflicts between nations. Instead the power struggles, for the most part, have been confined within national borders, albeit with international (and in particular superpower) involvement. And war has acquired a new dimension – terrorism.

As a result, governments have a free rein in subjugating dissidence. Very often questionable tactics are exercised in the name of law and order. The catalogue of violations against human rights is a long one – states of emergency that last for decades, imprisonment without trial, torture, the razing of villages and the burning of crops. The guerrilla armies too exact a terrible toll on the populace.

As the likelihood of war between nations diminishes, the savage nature of civil confrontation becomes more marked. For the most potent weapon in the hands of those who wage war is not chemical or nuclear, but the people in whose name and for whose good they claim they are fighting. Civilians have become the prime target, and their terror the means for domination. It is a theme that is played out in different versions in each of the following chapters.

The calculated use of force against civilians has mushroomed during the twentieth century. The process began in World War I with aerial bombardment and the indiscriminate use of mustard gas. After World War II, we saw slaughter during the partition of India, civilian massacres inflicted by both sides during Algeria's struggle for independence and the continuing bloody feuds in Northern Ireland. Television footage of the famine in Nigeria's civil war shocked the western world, as did coverage of Ethiopians starving to death in 1984. The agony never ends.

But we have seen so many pictures that the threshold of boredom is quickly crossed. Continuous exposure has made us immune to the suffering of those who live far away, do not look like us, and who are engulfed by causes we do not fully understand. Are we, too, not guilty in some small part through our inaction?

An unkind cynic once said that Texas went from barbarism to decadence without an intervening stage of civilization. Looking at the world today, it appears that many regions have gone from barbarism to barbarism with an intervening period of civilization.

It is as if the moment we relax our fight for control over the darker side of our nature, our ethics dissolve. Like liberty, the price of morality is eternal vigilance. Academics, philosophers and ordinary, caring people can argue and worry for hours, trying to pinpoint the agent of our moral erosion. Here it is enough to know that millions of people have become its victim. But how to stop this?

The International Committee of the Red Cross (ICRC), based in Switzerland, has long been a wellspring of action in the fight to protect civilians during war. The organization was founded in 1863 through the efforts of Henri Dunant, a visionary young Swiss. The idea came to him when he was caught up in a battle between the armies of Imperial Austria and the Franco-Sardinian alliance near Solferino, a small village in northern Italy. The casualties numbered about 40,000, a startling figure even by today's standards. There were virtually no military medical services, so Dunant organized the local people to bring relief to the wounded.

Dunant developed the Red Cross doctrine that wounded soldiers should be regarded as neutral, and that the protection that neutrality demanded should also be extended to the medical personnel who cared for them. This humanitarian principle was embellished and codified in the Geneva Convention. It gave an imprimatur to the notion that, war notwithstanding, the rule of law should be adhered to on and beyond the field of battle.

The moral wreckage left by World War II – the bombing of Hiroshima, Dresden and Coventry; the horrors of Auschwitz; the Katyn massacre – spurred on signatory states to extend the umbrella of protection. In 1949 they signed four new conventions that had been drawn up by the ICRC. The fourth convention concerned civilians. The ICRC's latest initiative is to draw the world's attention to the shocking nature of civilian casualties in the world today.

For many years the emblem of a red cross or crescent painted on an ambulance, or sewn on the shirts of thousands of dedicated men and women, was sufficient to guarantee the safe passage of ICRC workers. Not so any longer. Symbols are fragile protection and time has faded intent.

Almost without exception, governments involved in internal conflict consider it their own domain. There is increasing resistance to the presence of relief workers. In many countries they are accused, like the populace, of being 'terrorist sympathizers'. The same holds true for independent observers who monitor atrocities, such as journalists or representatives of human rights organizations. Increasingly, the people who could bring food and medicine to the conflict zones are prevented from doing so by governments that wish to bring armed opposition to its knees through hunger and disease.

Many of the people who manage to operate from behind rebel lines do so at very great risk to themselves. Sometimes their efforts end in tragedy. In October 1990 Peter Altwegg, an ICRC worker, was shot dead in an ambush in Somalia. He was travelling in a police vehicle when it was attacked by members of the rebel Somali National Movement. ICRC workers normally travel in their own vehicles, but on this occasion Altwegg's car had broken down and he had no other means of transport.

The chapter on Liberia highlights the difficulty of operating in the midst of lawlessness. ICRC workers were threatened and Medecins sans Frontières doctors came under fire from the army despite being given official clearance to travel on the roads.

The record for journalists is equally horrific. In 1989, fifty-three journalists were killed. Only seven of them were foreigners to the areas where they were reporting. Armed men will go far to deter open and fair reporting.

The imperatives of geopolitics, economics and ideology, combined with the prosperous arms trade and government reluctance to object to another government's actions, all contribute to the victimization of civilians.

The weapons of warfare are increasingly cruel, blind and unpredictable. Physically and mentally, innocent people are being mutilated under the illusion that methods of terror will ensure rapid and decisive victory. Of course, they do not.

Though conflicts may be contained within national borders, their consequences are not. The world is a global village. The problems of underdevelopment, famine, overpopulation, pollution and nuclear weapons are everyone's problems. In the same way as the burning down of a farm threatens an entire village, so today's anarchy places the entire planet in jeopardy. The remedy lies in concerted action. It is up to us, as citizens of the universe, to protest.

During the hunting season in Sweden, beaters and hunters wear a red stripe on their hats. It says, 'Hello! I am not an elk. I am a human being. Don't shoot me.' In one way, the present situation is no more complicated than that. Civilians have the right to insist, 'I have nothing to do with what you are doing. You must not kill me or destroy my life.'

In the final analysis, all of us are responsible for the victimization of others. It is up to us to decide whether or not the massacre of the innocent continues. If you are not convinced, this book may change your mind. It contains some very good reasons why we should act now. And supporting the International Committee of the Red Cross campaign to protect the victims of war would be a good place to start.

ETHIOPIA
THE SCORCHED EARTH
Mary Anne Fitzgerald

For thirty years the people of northern Ethiopia have been caught in a cycle of civil strife and drought that has killed over 1.5 million. Ethiopia has the second largest refugee population in the world.

It was the sort of day that lulled you into a false sense of security. The sky was overcast, sandwiching a strip of gentian blue between cloud and the russet mesas that rimmed the horizon. Difficult weather for fighter jets flying low on reconnaissance. The sort of day, in other words, that tempted people to walk outside, to go about their business as they used to twenty years ago when there was no war.

Small groups of men strode along tracks that hoofs had turned to dust, wrapped in brown rags and anxiety. From afar they looked like pilgrims, cast adrift from medieval times, as they glided across the windless plain.

Some drove thimble-footed donkeys before them, urging them on with wooden staves. The empty sacks slung across the animals' narrow backs were covered with eucalyptus branches. It was pitiful camouflage against the MiGs that regularly bombed the villages and towns. Sometimes the pilots even dropped bombs on men as they stood in their fields. But if you were a farmer who had never travelled in a car, let alone a plane, you were not to know that these green leaves carefully spread across burlap were useless.

These men had covered thirty miles and more in their tattered shammas and plastic sandals, marching across the flat-topped mountains. They had been entrusted with a weighty mission on which depended the survival of those family members who had not already died.

Their destination was the tiny market town of Idga Hamus in Tigray Province where, in the shelter of darkness, sacks of grain would be rationed out in a warehouse that night. They walked in silence, for energy must be conserved when you are malnourished. Even so, the promise of food for the first time in three months put a spring into their long strides.

In the vanguard of this expedition were Gebremehdin and his eldest son. Earlier that afternoon the two men had set off from Saessi, a cluster of flat-roofed homesteads perched atop a cliff. Like other villages, Saessi bore many trappings of the Iron Age. Some of the men still ploughed their fields with metal-tipped sticks. Water was collected from a hand-dug well. In the years when there were any, the harvests were stored in huge clay pots.

Gebremehdin had left his wife and six other children squatting listlessly in the sunlight by their house. In the last two weeks they had eaten only leaves and grass and wild seeds that had blown on to the fields. This bitter diet was hard to digest, and on some days they had eaten nothing at all. The old and the young – the most vulnerable age groups – were already dying. By the time Gebremehdin returned, his mother probably would not need the food he would bring strapped to the back of their donkey. She lay in the shadows in the darkened interior of the mud house beneath a row of cow horns. The makeshift hooks were the family's only possessions, apart from farming implements.

This dark bundle of rags lifted herself obligingly but with great effort on to one elbow to greet me when I stepped inside. Slowly she tipped her head forward a fraction. It was the merest suggestion of the courtly bow that was the standard Ethiopian greeting to strangers and friends alike.

It was so easy to read of scenes like this in the newspapers or to watch them on television. But it was difficult to stand there and look into the still eyes that presaged death by starvation. The courtyard outside was as quiet as a tomb. Even the shrunken baby, whose skin hung in folds, did not cry. Was it acceptance or resignation that enfolded this family?

Perhaps the key to survival was the people's bedrock faith in God. The domed churches of the Ethiopian Orthodox Church were to be found every

BELOW

During the 1985 famine, Tigrayan peasants walked for days to reach emergency relief centres. Their makeshift camps formed tableaux of despair.

where. Lepers and hunchbacks with carunculated limbs and stunted bodies congregated at their entrances, patiently waiting to be cured. Old men in the traditional garb of turban and jodhpurs and women swathed in white cotton cloth stopped to pray at the closed gates. They gripped the bars, touching them with their foreheads, kissing the metal intently. Like the beggars, they were hoping for a miracle to end their agony.

There were no beggars at the church near Gebremehdin's home, where tin bells tinkled in the breeze. Instead, beneath a cedar tree were two deep pits that had been hacked out of the stony ground. The men had dug these mass graves while they still had the strength to do so. Very soon they would be filled.

The year was 1990 when once again a miasma of despair had settled over the northern highlands. The harvests had been blighted by what the Western relief officials considered the worst drought in living memory. With hunger, disease and even locust plagues endemic, hyperbole was unnecessary. There was every possibility that over four million people would shrivel to that bicycle-chain thinness that had become Ethiopia's hallmark.

In the great drought five years earlier, when the rains failed and crops withered, more than a million died before the aid agencies mounted a massive relief operation. This time round the toll of human lives threatened to be even greater because efforts at food distribution had been crippled by conflict.

Contrary to popular opinion, the famine was not the result of poor farming methods. It was the product of one of Africa's oldest and bloodiest civil wars. The centrifugal force for this rebellion sprang from Tigray, the province most severely afflicted by drought.

Long before a military-led coup in 1974 extinguished the dynastic rule of Emperor Hailie Selassie and installed a new government, guerrilla activity was already crackling like popcorn in a pan. The opposition intensified under the rule of President Mengistu Haile Mariam.

Over the past year the insurgency had escalated into a full-scale war waged by the Ethiopian People's Revolutionary Democratic Front and the Eritrean People's Liberation Front. The bulk of the guerrillas in the EPRDF were from Tigray. They had vowed to overthow Mengistu.

Meanwhile, the people were trapped in a no man's land while the two sides fought each other with every modern weapon they could lay their hands on. A sinister war machine was steamrolling back and forth across the carcass of a ravaged land.

BELOW RIGHT

Tears of hunger are a good sign. During the final stages of malnutrition children are too weak to cry.

Fierce fighting had sealed off the foreign relief agencies' access to the drought-affected areas. The road that led north from the capital was clogged with busloads of soldiers going up to bolster the army's troops. Coming the other way was a stream of refugees from the turmoil: civil servants with beds tied to the roofs of their cars and fresh-faced aid workers who had been recalled to base. Ethiopia was engulfed in a maelstrom of famine and war.

Even though the airforce was blanketing the rebel bands of foot soldiers with cluster bombs, a deep loathing drove them on. Each battle left thousands dead and wounded. Often many of the casualties were civilians who had nowhere to hide, except in their fragile mud and stick huts. So great was the carnage that hyenas had developed a taste for human flesh and, for the first time that people could remember, were devouring the corpses that littered the plains.

The farmers were the true victims of this little-understood conflict. The Tigrayans had been tilling their precipitous mountains for 2,000 years, long

RIGHT
A priest holds an elaborate bronze cross as he reads from the Kidan (New Testament) in the doorway of a church chiselled out of rock.

LEFT
Christianity was introduced as the state religion in the fourth century. Here priests have gathered beneath an awning to chant mystical poetry to the accompaniment of drums and jingling metal rattles.

❝ Perhaps the key to survival was the people's bedrock faith in God. The domed churches of the Ethiopian Orthodox Church were to be found everywhere. Lepers and hunchbacks... congregated at their entrances, patiently waiting to be cured. ❞

before agriculture had taken hold in Europe. Over the centuries they had mastered sound agricultural practices.

Before the guerrillas had succeeded in driving the army out of Tigray the previous year, troops had roamed the countryside deliberately butchering plough oxen and destroying farm tools. They set fire to fields of ripening sorghum and barley and torched the grain stored in huts. A complex peasant economy, developed over centuries, had been torn apart. For the past six months they had been surviving on occasional supplies of wheat and lentils distributed by the rebel-run Relief Society of Tigray. But the flow of food was drying to a trickle. Western governments were reluctant to support the rebels, even though the cause was a humanitarian one. Donated emergency rations had to be transported for 600 miles across the border from Sudan.

The ancient trucks crawled along pot-holed roads that first crossed the dusty lowlands, then negotiated hairpin bends stitched to the sides of mountains.

LEFT

In contrast to previous famines, when millions trekked for days or weeks in search of food, farmers such as this man were told to stay in their villages so that they could prepare their fields for the next planting season.

ABOVE

In 1985 the countryside was emptied of people as they flocked to feeding camps, seeking food handouts and medicine that kept some, but not all, alive. Over a million died.

Before the pink rays of dawn had spread across the sky, they were already nestled under thorn trees, covered with tattered sacks and tarpaulins to escape detection from the air.

I knew only too well the danger that attended the daylight hours. I had travelled into Tigray with a photographer and a two-man television crew in a convoy carrying wheat and lentils. At the end of each bone-shaking, twelve-hour trek, we brushed away our tyre tracks in the sandy river beds and crawled under thorn bushes. The long, heat-filled hours oozed along like treacle as we fended off the flies and inquisitive goats.

One morning our routine was shattered. The eleven trucks had been hidden beneath a canopy of trees in a deep gully. We were bivouacked a few miles outside Sherraro, an insignificant cluster of shops and houses draped in an early morning mist. At 10.15 two MiG-21s screamed over our heads and bombarded the town while the terrified residents took refuge in crude earth shelters dug into the ground.

LEFT

A Tigrayan woman in the trappings of war wears a dress made from a grain sack and holds an AK-47 automatic rifle. Women forgo marriage to become fighters when they are fifteen and make up about one fifth of the rebel force.

RIGHT

Tigrayan peasants congregate at a rebel-run food distribution centre tucked into a gully on the side of a mountain. The area was so remote that it was considered safe from aerial bombing attacks by the government's MiG jet fighters. Elsewhere food distribution was carried out under the cover of darkness.

LEFT

Soldiers of the Ethiopian People's Revolutionary Democratic Front scan the precipitous terrain that is under rebel control.

‘ Beneath a cedar tree were two deep pits that had been hacked out of the stony ground. The men had dug these mass graves while they still had the strength to do so. Very soon they would be filled. ’

Suspected as a depot for relief supplies, the airforce searched the area up to six times a day. Their cat's paw attacks had already destroyed 270 houses.

To our dismay, the MiGs returned at 3.15 that afternoon. The carefully camouflaged vehicles were almost invisible. But perhaps a wing mirror had not been bent close enough to the door, giving a tell-tale glint as it reflected the sun. Or perhaps a government spy had reported our presence. In the end, the manner of betrayal did not matter.

The circling jets banked and dived steeply, flattening out over the gully to blanket our convoy with high explosive and phosphorous bombs. They systematically pounded the vehicles for half an hour. We took refuge in a peasant's house and watched the livid flashes and dark grey towers of smoke in horror.

A third attack ninety minutes later took us by surprise. I ran across a field of stubble and dived for cover behind an anthill. Villagers who had rushed to assess the damage were trapped in the gully. The photographer, James Hamilton, was amongst them. They ran screaming, their mouths torn wide with fear, dodging the explosions and cannon fire that ripped along the banks.

A quarter of the convoy and four tons of precious grain were destroyed that day. Miraculously, there was only one casualty: he was a thirty-seven-year-old herder called Weldegerima whose stomach was ripped apart by shrapnel as he ran to save his cattle. He died in agony minutes later without benefit of first aid or benediction. I squatted beside him, my hand encircling his storklike wrist as I swatted the flies from his face. It was a futile attempt to ease his last moments.

It was to see food handed out that brought us to Idga Hamus two weeks later on the day the sky was the merest strip of gentian. Standing on the outskirts of the town was a U-shaped building of dressed stone. Its courtyard was filled with barefoot women whose braided hair fanned out at the nape of the neck like peacock plumage. They were surrounded by silent children, folded sunshades and clumps of geraniums and orange marigolds.

In two sparsely-furnished rooms Sisters Bernadette and Theresa of the Little Sisters of the Assumption were tending shrunken babies who had the translucent faces of very old men on their deathbeds. Both the nuns were from Ireland, smiling, good-natured women well into their fifties, perhaps older. They were the only foreigners in the area. With the help of Ethiopian nurses, they attended to the medical needs of some 10,000 people.

LEFT

When starvation is endemic, mothers give their rations to the older children and let the babies die.

ABOVE RIGHT

The 1985 feeding camps were so crowded that those who died during the night could not be extricated until morning when they were taken to a special tent to be prepared for burial.

RIGHT

Disinfected and wrapped in rags, a mother and child await the grave.

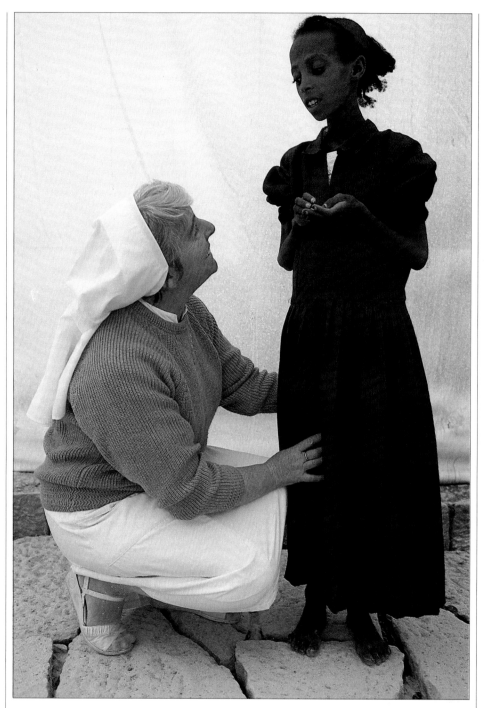

❛ **The scenes were a cameo of the political imbroglio, an epitaph for the *Angst* that had forced brother to betray brother and cousin to kill cousin. ❜**

The sisters lived on their own in a building next door. Hanging in the small living room was a sign that said, 'The cost of 1 jet fighter = 40,000 village health clinics.' The stone rooms surrounded a haphazard garden planted with parsley, tomatoes, potatoes, geraniums, petunias and marigolds. 'This is where we vent our anger and frustration, but we don't have time now,' said Theresa.

I offered to help by sowing a packet of beetroot seeds. It was a laborious job. The pick was crudely made and the earth hard and rocky. Malnourished and debilitated by dysentery, I stopped every few minutes to recoup my strength.

Bernadette came to join me as I sat on a stone catching my breath. She was a tiny woman, not more than 5 ft 2 in tall, but she tackled her job with the courage and determination of a terrier. At that moment two MiG-23 fighter jets screamed past. They circled once and then again, dipping their wings so that the pilots could take a closer look at the people who had chosen this cloudy day to walk abroad.

I tried to control my fear but could not. Bernadette stood stock still, her head thrown back. Involuntarily, I clasped her hand. 'They're circling twice. That means they're going to drop something,' she said in a matter-of-fact voice.

I knew it was useless to hide, but could not bear to witness more tragedy. When Bernadette suggested we go to her bedroom, I nodded my head as if in a dream. She produced a set of gaoler's keys and slowly tried each one in turn. 'Wouldn't you know it. You always get the wrong key when you're in a hurry.'

We sat on her bed while she pointed out the pictures of her nieces and nephews in Dublin that hung on the wall, talking to distract my attention from the planes overhead. Providence was on our side that day. As she showed me her few possessions – some pearl soap in a shell-shaped dish and two glass swans – we could hear the jets roar into the distance to continue their search for rebel troops somewhere else.

Two years earlier, Bernadette had been awoken late at night by a banging on the door. The rebels took her away and forced her to march through the mountains for six days in her red wool dressing gown. She did not know why she had been seized nor if she was going to be killed, because none of the men in the group spoke English.

Later, she discovered the kidnapping was a stunt to demonstrate how exhausting it was for the Tigrayans, in the grip of another famine, to walk for days to reach the government-run food distribution centres. This time, thanks to the widespread network of the Relief Society of Tigray, most farmers spent no more than a day fetching emergency rations.

'I can't explain it to the other nuns, but there's always a fear that I'll be taken away again,' Bernadette confided. 'Still, after I was shipped home when I was ill, I chose to come back again. They are so used to being abandoned. It meant a lot to them when I returned. They brought me eggs and baskets they had woven. They were dirty by the time they got to me, but that didn't matter. I don't leave for another two years, and who knows what might happen by then. With all these MiGs about, every day is a bonus.'

Like Bernadette, the Tigrayans were gentle and friendly. It was difficult to understand why they should have invoked suffering of such awesome proportions. But the carapace of what appeared to the outsider as indifference was easier to comprehend.

One afternoon we replayed for rebel officials some footage the televison team had taken. The film was of a battle in which villagers hiding in a storm drain took a direct hit from a bomb. The harrowing images depicted barefoot men in sheepskin capes trying to shovel mangled bodies out of the earth. Women encased in grief danced a mindless jig beside their dead husbands.

The scenes were a cameo of the political imbroglio, an epitaph for the *Angst* that had forced brother to betray brother and cousin to kill cousin. The Tigrayans watched intently as the carnage unfolded on the tiny video screen. But afterwards they were silent.

'It's amazing, isn't it?' prodded the television reporter.

Teklewoini Assefa, the indefatigable field co-ordinator for the Relief Society of Tigray, suddenly looked very tired. 'You are shocked, but we have all seen scenes like this before,' he said. 'We have all lost friends and family. If we give vent to our emotions, we will be paralysed. We can't afford the luxury of feeling.'

> ❛ It was so easy to read of scenes like this in the newspapers or to watch them on television. But it was difficult to stand there and look into the still eyes that presaged death by starvation. ❜

Mary Anne Fitzgerald has been visiting Ethiopia for over twenty years. This story was written after she had spent some time travelling with the Tigrayan People's Liberation Front in February 1990.

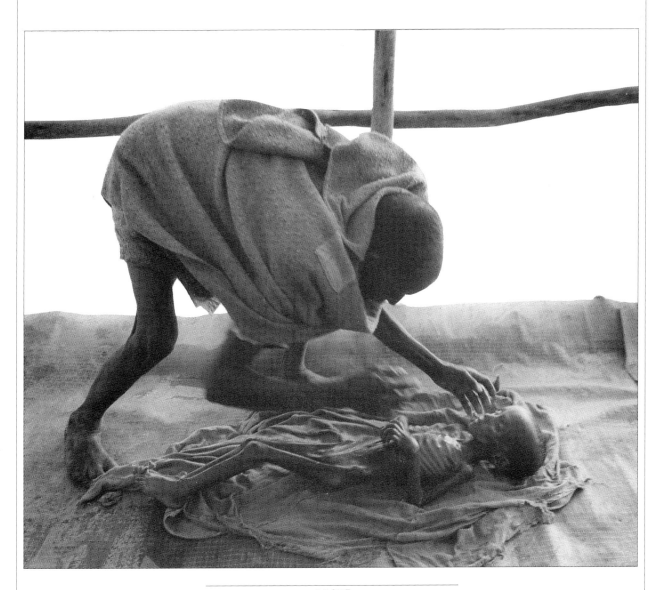

ABOVE

To the end, Ethiopians retain their dignity in the face of
tragedy. A father bids a tender farewell to his son as he
strokes his eyes shut.

LEFT

A couple and their baby ignore celebrations of the release from the Maze prison of a young Ballymurphy man. The local Girl Scout band gave a concert in front of his house while his comrades hijacked and burned a truck in his honour.

ABOVE

Rathlin Island encapsulates the peace and beauty of Northern Ireland's countryside.

NORTHERN IRELAND

A FAMILY AFFAIR

Alf McCreary

Conflict in Northern Ireland has been the norm for so long that it is almost impossible to remember, let alone pinpoint its origins. A recent increase in violence suggests that a peaceful solution remains elusive. Meanwhile no one, whether directly or through links of blood or friendship, is left untouched.

'The wall collapsed . . . and we were thrown forward . . . rubble and stones . . . all around us . . . I remember thinking, I'm not hurt, but there's a pain in my shoulder . . . we were under six feet of rubble . . . Then, almost by magic, I found my hand being squeezed, and I knew it was my daughter Marie. She gripped my right hand and asked, "Is that you Dad?" I could hardly believe that she was here, after all, lying beside me in the rubble . . . I shouted "How are you, Marie?" She replied, "I'm fine." My heart skipped a beat, with relief. But then, suddenly and terribly, she screamed. I knew that there must be something awfully wrong for her to scream like that. Again I asked her, "Are you all right?" . . . And again came the reply, "Yes." But there seemed to be a bit of hesitation in that Yes . . . Then she screamed again.

'It was her second scream. I became desperately concerned about Marie's condition. I could not and I still cannot, understand how she could keep reassuring me that she was fine and yet, in between these messages of reassurance, she was screaming. Whether they were screams of pain or of terror, I'll never know . . . It must have been four or five times I shouted to Marie, "Are you all right?" But then, suddenly, her voice changed, she sounded different. She held my hand tightly, and gripped me as hard as she could. She said, "Daddy, I love you very much." Those were her exact words to me, and those were the last words I ever heard her say. . .'

The story of Gordon Wilson and the death of his beloved daughter Marie, a student nurse of twenty, penetrates the hardest of hearts. His words convey the agony and suffering of the people of Northern Ireland who have been trapped for two decades in the brutal and apparently unending cycle of violence in that so green and beautiful country. Gordon Wilson and Marie had left their house on a Sunday morning to attend the Remembrance Day service at the Cenotaph in Enniskillen, a small country town of considerable character nestling among the picturesque lakes of Fermanagh on the northern side of the Irish border. They bade goodbye to Mrs Joan Wilson who asked, 'Have you got your umbrella, Marie?' She replied, 'Of course I have. Don't fuss!' That was the last Joan saw of Marie until she lay dying in the Erne Hospital later that afternoon.

❝ Whatever the rights and wrongs, brutality is the daily reality of this tortured land. ❞

Masked rioters are often teenagers, as in this prelude
to a riot in Derry. In the background are British Army
armoured personnel carriers.

In the meantime, a bomb planted by the Provisional IRA (Irish Republican Army) in a disused schoolhouse near the Cenotaph ripped the building apart, killing eleven civilians and maiming many others. It was one of the most horrific incidents in the already long and appalling catalogue of atrocities in Northern Ireland. Ordinary people in ordinary families in ordinary places were being torn wide open. And some were telling their story in an extraordinary way, like Joan Wilson.

'At the hospital we got out of the lift at Intensive Care. Sister met us and told us that Marie's heart was still beating, but it might stop at any minute. We turned into the room. The specialist who had been one of the many who had fought for her life in theatre was standing beside Marie's bed. He looked at us sadly, and shook his head. I could not believe that the girl who left our home at 10.20 a.m. so full of life and vitality was lying there with her life ebbing away. My darling Marie was dying. I kissed her and I shall always see her eyelids flickering to my dying day. Sister whispered very gently, "Mrs Wilson, Marie's

LEFT

Participants in riots such as this one in Derry wear masks to protect their identity. The black balaclava gives this man the air of an executioner.

heart has stopped beating." Julie Anne, our other daughter, took my hand and said, "Mum, it is better this way." I could only utter, "The Lord gave, the Lord has taken away. Blessed be the name of the Lord." I had to lean hard on the Lord now, he was my only strength. I had to go down and tell Gordon that his darling daughter was dead. I kept going back to look at Marie. I am sure I walked in and out of that little room six times or more, until Sister gently and very lovingly reminded me I had a duty to go downstairs, to tell Gordon.'

No father or mother could fail to be moved by such words of pain and loss. They are as universal as humanity itself. And yet the violence goes on and on.

October 1990 was a particularly terrible month. Among the many incidents of terror, three men were abducted from their homes by the IRA and forced to drive vehicles filled with explosives to British Army checkpoints.

Gerry Kelly managed to struggle free when he arrived at the Lisanelly army camp. John McEvoy escaped with a broken leg, but Cyril Smith, the Royal Irish Ranger who dragged him to safety, was killed by the explosion.

ABOVE

Bernadette McDonnell joins the protest for better conditions for prisoners, such as her father, who were being held in the Maze prison.

The third man, Patsy Gillespie, was blown apart when the 1,000 lb bomb behind him exploded. He was forty-two when he died and had worked for nearly fifteen years in the kitchens at an army camp. The explosion also killed five British soldiers. The horrific incident made a widow of his wife Kathleen. His twelve-year-old daughter, Jennifer, and two teenage sons, Patrick and Kieran, lost a father.

Kathleen told *Sunday Times* reporters: 'When we got home that night there were already five of them in the house, holding Jennifer in the front room. They wore casual clothes, and they all had trendy casual gear and jeans. They never produced a gun at any time. Their presence was enough.

'She was hysterical, but the men were calm and very professional and they said from the beginning that no harm would come to any of us. They just wanted to take Patsy away for a little while.

'They used my car and they let Patsy have a moment with us before they went. I will remember till the day I die what he was like. He put his arms around

LEFT

Children grow up fed on distorted moral values such as this West Belfast youth with a stocking over his head.

RIGHT

Large families and skimpy incomes mean that people struggle to keep up payments on the furniture from their dole. Children are lured into the ranks of the fighting to escape the hopelessness of unemployment and poverty.

❛ They killed him in cold blood even as they told me quietly he would be fine. They turned him into a human bomb and watched him being blown to pieces. ❜

Jennifer and me and said, "Don't worry. Everything will be OK. It's going to be fine." He was very pale, but in control. It was the last time I was ever to see him. But even though I was terrifed, I thought all the time he would be OK . . . It never dawned on me they were going to use him as a human bomb.

'After they left, three of the men stayed on, and about four hours went by. I thought the night would never end, but at 3.57 a.m. exactly the phone rang three times and then it stopped. The man walked over and ripped it from the wall. He said to us, "Don't you worry. Nobody is going to get hurt. Your husband will be home within the half hour." Then they walked out, closing the door silently.'

Some twelve hours later, the police called to let Kathleen know that her husband's body had been found in the carnage at the Coshquin road check. 'I felt such hate and revulsion. They killed him in cold blood even as they told me quietly he would be fine. They turned him into a human bomb and watched him being blown to pieces.'

RIGHT
A Catholic woman peers cautiously above the wreckage of the day's rioting stacked in front of her doorway to see if it is safe to go out.

RIGHT
A Catholic woman peers cautiously above the wreckage of the day's rioting stacked in front of her doorway to see if it is safe to go out.

❛ In towns and cities there is no guarantee of safety. A busy street can suddenly be transformed into a backdrop for murder. ❜

Fifty miles further south, on the same night, the IRA had hammered down the door of the isolated cottage where Gerry Kelly lived with his wife and seven-year-old daughter. 'It was the longest drive of my life. I realized I had to get there pretty quickly to keep within the time limit, but I was terrified of going too fast in case the vibrations set off the bomb.

'It seems you get caught up in all this madness whether you like it or not. I can sell the house OK, but I don't know where I'm going to go from here,' he said afterwards.

Much of the violence has been caused by the IRA, but not exclusively so. There is also violence from the loyalist Protestant terrorists. They were spawned as a reaction to IRA violence and have become a nasty mirror image of their enemy.

The police and British Army have used violence in the course of their duties too
– arrests, searches, rubber bullets, tear gas. Whatever the rights and wrongs,
brutality is the daily reality of this tortured land.

The rural peace of a lovely country hedgerow can be shattered by chattering
gunfire or the roar of highly explosive materials hidden under a road and
detonated by remote control. The noise subsides; the dirt settles; the dead and
injured are taken away; and a slow, uncertain peace returns to the watching and
waiting countryside.

In towns and cities there is no guarantee of safety. A busy street can suddenly
be transformed into a backdrop for murder. In Belfast one morning, two young
terrorists walked up to two police dog handlers and opened fire. They melted
into the crowd and escaped: one policeman died, the other was badly injured.

❛ There are areas of ghetto-type poverty where lack of job opportunities beget violence. For the bored youngsters who hang out at the betting shops, pubs and on the street corners, the ritual attacks against patrolling 'Brits' are tempting. **❜**

RIGHT & BELOW

Armed with sticks and stones, young boys join in the rioting.

The shooting took place on a street of banks, electrical stores, restaurants, boutiques: the kind of shops anyone frequents in any other city. The two policemen were left in pools of blood not far from a small café where, until recently, I used to breakfast each Saturday morning while my young son attended choir practice in a nearby church. If his choir practice had not been switched to a Friday, I might well have seen the policemen stagger to the ground as I finished my tea and toast.

The violence is swift and sudden. Then, like an evil shadow that has passed over the sun, it disappears. The screams of shoppers fade on the air. The traffic rumbles on. Two more people have become statistics.

War has been integrated into our culture for so long that youngsters under twenty have always known conflict. There are areas of ghetto-type poverty where lack of job opportunities beget violence. For the bored youngsters who hang out at the betting shops, pubs and on the street corners, the ritual attacks against patrolling 'Brits' are tempting. It is a generation which easily graduates into the ranks of the paramilitary organizations controlled by the 'Godfathers', who direct the violence from behind the scenes but are rarely apprehended.

It is a conflict that people take in their stride because they have no option. There is a sense of outrage, pity and despair. But it is human nature to look for the best, to bury the fear and the disgust as deep down as conscience will allow.

So we point out, rightly, that more people die in traffic accidents on our roads than in the Troubles. We tell you, correctly, that Northern Ireland has one of the best education systems in the world; that our coastline and forests and rivers and lakes are stupendously beautiful; that our people are generally open, warm and friendly; that we are attracting visitors and investors. But we cannot tell you if or when the terror will stop. And we would admit deep down that we are scarred by past tragedies and dread the prospect of more.

It is not easy to live with this personal yet communal grief. You are not sure about confiding in your neighbour in case he has a different point of view. So we all suffer according to our various thresholds of pain in this province which seems fated to re-run endlessly the gauntlet of war.

BELOW

Like father, like son. Children play war games in the back streets of Londonderry.

Who can really understand Northern Ireland, even if they want to? The conflict is not about religion itself, despite outward appearances. It is about identity and precisely whether Northern Ireland wants to remain British or to become more Irish or stay as a mixture of both. The majority of the roughly one million Protestants want to stay British. Most of the half million Roman Catholics favour an Ireland united through peaceful means. The debate has been ignited into conflagration by several hundred active members of the IRA and the Loyalists, with the security forces caught in the middle.

However, I remain hopeful, perhaps blindly, defiantly and stubbornly so, inspired by the courage of ordinary people.

My thoughts focus on Jennifer McNern, who lost both legs in an explosion at the Abercorn Restaurant in Belfast, and also on her sister Rosaleen, who lost both legs and an arm in the same blast. The two sisters learnt what the word casualty really meant during the months they spent in tidy wards amid the quiet routine of hospital life.

After a few months they were fitted with artificial limbs. They had to learn to walk inch by inch, holding on to parallel bars. It was not easy and required enormous grit and determination. But they did make progress.

They then learned to move around strapped on to walking aids called pylon rockers. They shuffled forward in a curious rocking motion rather like a duck.

BELOW

People flee in panic during the Milltown cemetery massacre. A Loyalist paramilitary shot three people dead and injured many others when he sought revenge amongst mourners at an IRA funeral.

A masked rioter in Londonderry.

BELOW RIGHT

Catholic demonstrators hijacked a car, parked it in the entranceway to a British fort and set it on fire. When the British Army dispatched an armoured front loader to remove the flaming barricade, the demonstrators attacked it with petrol bombs.

Because they were in hospital, no one paid any attention to the fact that they were half normal size. It was an emotional moment when they saw themselves for the first time at their usual height.

'You told yourself, "This is it. This is the way you will have to go for the rest of your life." It wasn't really all that bad when you thought about it,' Jennifer told me later.

The girls refused to succumb to self-pity. Even when they were in hospital, they insisted on putting on their make-up and wearing pretty clothes. Within a year of leaving hospital, Rosaleen married Brendan Murrin, whom she had met as a teenager.

They were married by her cousin from New York, Father Cornelius Blaney. His final blessing referred to the future, not to the past, and could have been for any young couple starting life together: 'May you have children to bless you, friends to console you, and may you live in peace with all men.'

Jimmy Hughes lost his legs in the same blast. One afternoon, as he was sitting on his stumps, he asked me, 'How's life?' From my height of six feet plus, I told him about my irritations of the day. Almost as an afterthought I said, 'How are you?' He replied quietly, 'Oh, I can't complain.'

> **❝ The violence is swift and sudden. Then, like an evil shadow that has passed over the sun, it disappears. The screams of shoppers fade on the air. The traffic rumbles on. Two more people have become statistics. ❞**

LEFT

The Falls Road is the centrepiece of working-class Catholic life. A woman goes about her business oblivious to her surroundings, while a British soldier scans a building through the sights of his rifle. A hijacked vehicle burns in the background.

There is also my friend Maura Kiely, a devout Roman Catholic mother who almost lost her faith and her senses when her son Gerard, a student, was shot dead on the steps of a church by an assailant still unknown. Maura was so distraught she threw a cup of coffee over a picture of Christ. She said, 'I was almost at the stage where I was asking God to forgive God. I was so angry.' But Maura's faith did not break. She survived, and now helps to run a group for other bereaved people. Occasionally we meet at conferences and we hug each other. But we both know that the pain will never totally go away.

When history is written, I will not ask who won. For I know we have all lost. I will remember the anguish of Kathleen Gillespie, a Catholic, and the last words of Marie Wilson, a Protestant, as she lay dying under the rubble at Enniskillen. 'Daddy, I love you very much.' And I shall ask God to forgive us all.

Alf McCreary is an award-winning journalist, author and broadcaster who lives in Northern Ireland. Four of his eleven books are about victims of violence. His latest book, Marie – A Story from Enniskillen, *was written with Gordon Wilson and published by Marshall Pickering.*

RIGHT

A Belfast building in flames hits the street despite the efforts of a lone fireman.

CAMBODIA
BETWEEN THE TIGER & THE CROCODILE
Patrice de Beer

Cambodia has experienced more than two decades of genocide. Between 1970 and 1973 the United States dropped more bombs on Cambodia than on Germany during World War II. Some two million people died in Cambodia's forced labour camps and interrogation centres under the Khmer Rouge in the late 1970s. Now, in a renewed civil war, over 100,000 people have been maimed by landmines.

When Phnom Penh woke up on the hot and muggy morning of 17 April 1975, the capital was eerily still. Long columns of sun-baked Khmer Rouge guerrillas were marching in single file down its wide avenues, as silent as ghosts. General Lon Nol's soldiers had laid down their arms and most of his followers had fled during the night. The bloody fighting of the past five years seemed to have come to an end. It was, in fact, the prelude to four years of Khmer Rouge-inspired terror. Most of the victims of the holocaust of the carpet-bombings, famine, slaughter, and, yes, cannibalism too, had been civilians. Exhausted by a brutal conflict that had displaced millions and killed hundreds of thousands, Cambodians thought that the nightmare was now over.

Half of the country's seven million population had sought refuge in Phnom Penh, surviving on food handouts brought in with great difficulty by the ICRC and voluntary agencies along the Mekong river. After the Khmer Rouge closed the river earlier in the year, rice and medicine had continued to trickle in by means of an erratic and risky airlift.

A team of Red Cross doctors and nurses who had manned the hospitals up to the last minute of the war were herded into the former French Embassy when the capital fell. They were kept there for two weeks and then expelled to Thailand with the rest of the foreigners.

Trapped with them in the compound, I witnessed the last days of the war. I was among those who bade farewell to Dith Pran, the hero of *The Killing Fields*, when he walked through the gates to mix with the flow of refugees. It was a heart-rending moment. But the worst had yet to come.

Phnom Penh's optimism soon proved to be chimerical. The city that had successfully managed to shelter so many from atrocities now spewed them forth. No one knew it at the time, but they were being propelled towards a genocide on a scale that had not been visited on a people since the partial exterminations of the Jews and the Armenians.

A few hours after being welcomed as victors, the Khmer Rouge, some of them gun-toting teenagers who had never seen a town before, started to evict

ABOVE

Buddhist monks framed in an ornately decorated window. This photograph was taken in the early 1970s. Thousands of monks were executed by Khmer Rouge troops a few years later.

LEFT

The templed city of Angkor Wat dates back to the early twelfth century. Fighting has ebbed and flowed around its perimeter, but the buildings have survived.

❝ Living skeletons were marched from one end of Cambodia to the other, leaving the paths littered with corpses. ❞

A man who lost his leg on a landmine hops down a
Phnom Penh street.

ABOVE

Dith Pran, the photographer whose harrowing
experiences under the Khmer Rouge were recounted in
The Killing Fields, is reunited with his aunt Meak Oth on
a return trip to Cambodia.

patients and staff from the hospitals and families from their homes. Sometimes they did it with a grin on their faces, more often at gunpoint. The city was engulfed in panic.

A group of young guerrillas dressed in black pyjamas knocked at Mr Ly Chheng Eav's door. Their heads were wrapped in the traditional Khmer scarf, the *kramar*. He was given only a few minutes to pack some belongings and leave his shop with his wife, young children and aged mother.

They joined the thousands, perhaps millions, who were thronging the avenues, carrying small bundles of hastily gathered food and possessions. The rich, unaware of what lay ahead, drove their Mercedes Benz and Citroëns Deux Chevaux. There was very little petrol in the beleaguered city, and some had to push their cars. The people were dazed, stunned as they walked along the heat-filled streets that steamed from the early monsoon rains. Some pushed carts carrying old people and wailing children. Some wrestled with hospital beds that held sick or wounded relatives.

BELOW

Dith Pran visits one of the mass graves that testify to the genocide he managed to escape. This building on the road to Angkor Wat had been wrecked by artillery shelling in the early Seventies. When the fighting was over, people dug up the corpses and stacked the skulls on a table.

❝ No one knew it at the time, but they were being propelled towards a genocide on a scale that had not been visited on a people since the partial exterminations of the Jews and the Armenians. ❞

Families were separated in the mêlée and children were lost. Soon bags and cars were abandoned while those who were too tired or too old to keep up were left by the side of the road. Some were shot where they lay.

It took days to empty the city and weeks for the Lys to reach their destination, a grassy patch of land on the edge of a jungle. Like the other townspeople, who had never lived in the country, they were forced to build a shack to live in, to become rice farmers and to work with their hands for the first time.

The guerrillas had told them the move was temporary and they would soon be allowed to go back to Phnom Penh. In fact, it would be four years before Mr Ly could return to his devastated home. He was luckier than millions of others who were claimed for ever by these killing fields.

Instead of suturing old wounds, the cataclysmic events that took place after the fall of Phnom Penh tore the nation apart. Cities were reclaimed by the jungle or became overgrown with banana trees. The rice paddies that once fed the people were turned into concentration camps and, very soon, graveyards.

Mr Ly and his wife managed to survive, his mother and children did not. He saw his neighbours ferreted out and accused of being traitors, betrayed by their soft hands and reading glasses. Some were suffocated in plastic bags. Others were clubbed or hacked to death.

Mr Ly worked from sunrise to late at night, digging canals and building dams. As with the others in this tropical gulag, he subsisted on one or two tins of rice gruel a day. Sometimes he managed to forage a few leaves as well. From the start, he had been separated from his family, so each night he slept for a few hours in a communal tin shed with the other men.

The inhabitants of these forced labour camps were stripped of even the most basic of the rituals that differentiate animals from human beings. They were forbidden to cook anything for themselves, they were not allowed to grow anything, or own anything. Gone too were the trappings normally associated with ordinary civilization – education, medicine, religion, money, compassion and kindness.

RIGHT
The post-operative recovery room in the civilian hospital at Kompong Thom in central Cambodia.

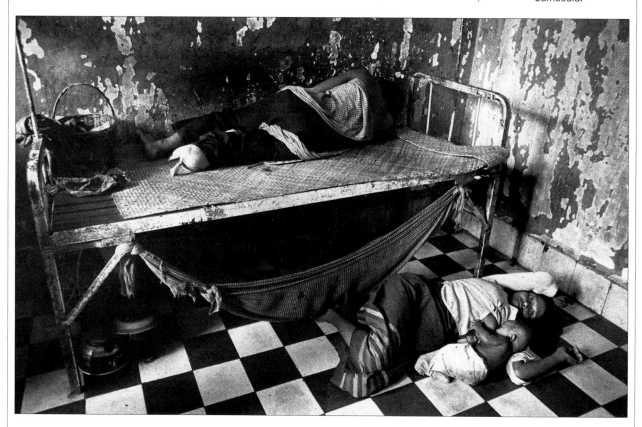

ABOVE
The post-surgery ward in the Sleam Reap hospital. An average of two people a day are admitted suffering from mine wounds.

All too soon the effects of deprivation began to mow down the prisoners like a giant scythe. The men could not work without food. Hunger made the women sterile. The children died like flies from disease. Living skeletons were marched from one end of Cambodia to the other, leaving the paths littered with corpses. The Khmer Rouge vision of an Asian supernation withered. They dreamt of the population growing to twenty million. Instead, their barbarism decimated it. It is possible that half the Cambodian population died in those four years.

For those who returned afterwards, as I did in 1981, Tuol Sleng is an obligatory visit. Once it was a secondary school in a plush residential area in Phnom Penh. Today it is a museum. In the interim it was Cambodia's Auschwitz.

The walls of Tuol Sleng are still topped with barbed wire, an intimation of what lies within. Its sinister reputation envelops you as you cross the courtyards to go from one building to the next.

The Khmer Rouge turned the schoolrooms into cells of interrogation, torture and killing. This was where the Khmer Rouge tortured their own party

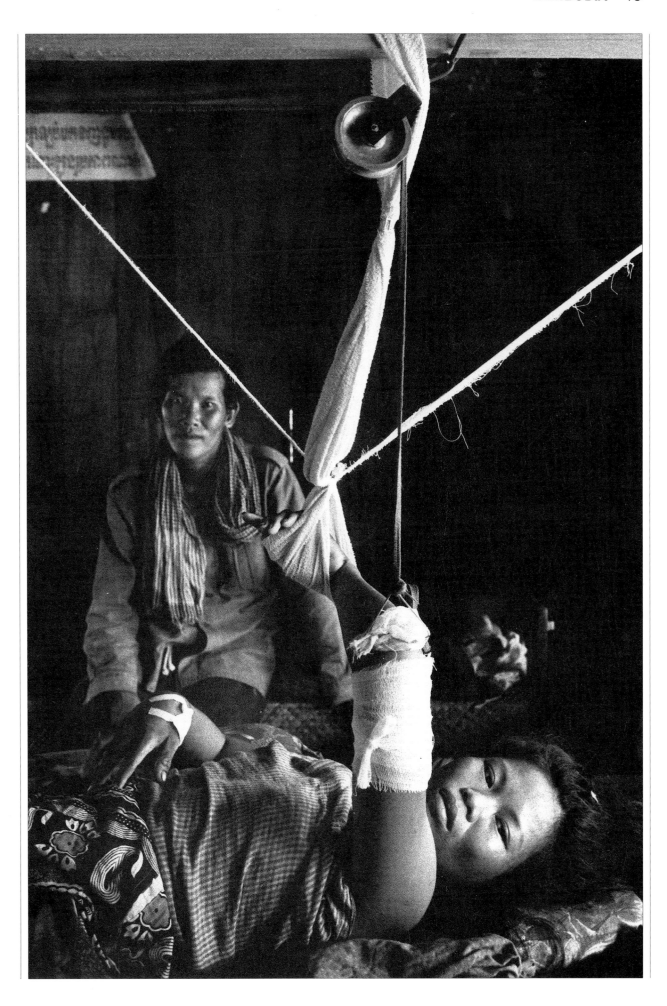

LEFT

The victims of Tuol Sleng were photographed twice. On arrival as a means of identity, and when they left as corpses to prove to Khmer Rouge leaders that they had been eliminated. Some smiled in the initial picture, not knowing what lay ahead.

BELOW

Once Tuol Sleng was a secondary school in a smart residential area. Today it is a museum. In the interim it was Cambodia's Auschwitz.

RIGHT

A visitor to the Museum of the Genocidal Crimes of Pol Pot at Tuol Sleng examines photographs of some of the 20,000 people who were put to death there.

people, forcing them to denounce family and colleagues. Their paranoia about traitors in their midst was boundless. It would have seemed that the enemy within was a greater threat than the enemy without. The maw of death was insatiable and undiscriminating.

I entered a room that was bare except for an iron bed where the victims were laid out and forced to denounce their families and confess their sins. In front of it was a desk and one chair. What lesson did the interrogators think they were teaching? And what lesson do these stark rooms now hold for mankind?

Many of the visitors to the museum go there to search for the face of a lost relative amongst the rows and rows of prints that hang on the walls. The photographs were taken on two occasions – when people arrived as a form of identification, and when the corpses left as proof to party leaders that they had been killed. Some people smiled for their first photograph because they had no idea what lay ahead. Others stood there with their hands tied behind their backs, numbers pinned to their shirts, their eyes bulging with fear. Visitors are visibly shaken when they walk out into the sunshine. The museum is a testimony to the desecration of Cambodia's heritage.

About 20,000 people were put to death at Tuol Sleng under the Khmer Rouge regime. Evil cannot be quantified, but if the murders took place every day of the week and every week of the year, then about fifteen people died every single day. It is a grim record.

When they managed to flee Cambodia, the survivors told gruesome stories. They were so gruesome that no one believed them at first. Some were so frightened they refused to give their names, fearing that retribution would hunt them down no matter where they hid. Others, like Dith Pran, courageously excavated memories and testified to their nightmares.

Yim Sot Tannaki escaped to Thailand in February 1978. He was the sole survivor of a massacre of seventy-six people. The Khmer Rouge had come to

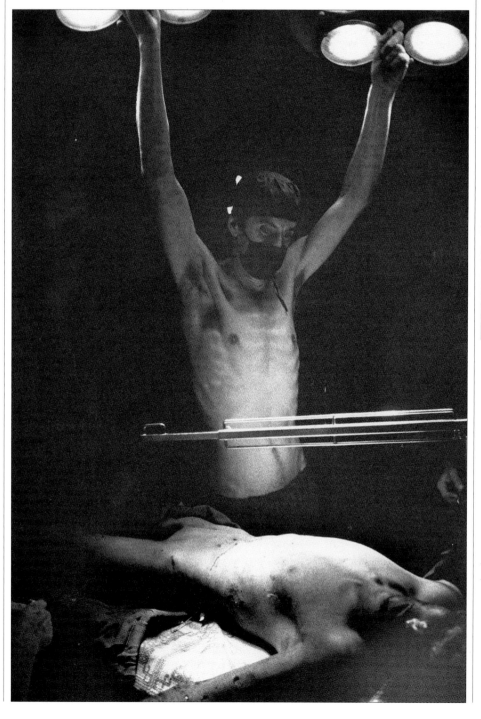

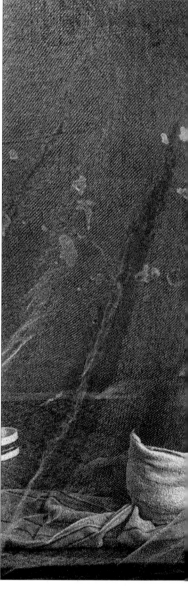

ABOVE

A Cambodian boy recuperates after having half his leg amputated. At the beginning of the rainy season patients are covered with mosquito nets to keep out swarming flies that would infect the wounds.

LEFT

Doctor Bruno Dehaye, a surgeon working for the French humanitarian organization, Medecins sans Frontières, adjusts his lamps before operating on Mr Heng Chu, a farmer who was injured by a mine while ploughing his field.

> **Those who finally made it to the refugee camps in Thailand were nothing more than skeletons. The aim of the game seemed to be to control not just the territory but also the people. They were the pawns of war.**

his village in Eastern Siem-Reap Province and accused the men of being traitors. They were marched into the jungle and hit on the back of the head with shovels. The Khmer Rouge did not like to waste bullets.

'I heard people screaming. My brother fell beside me. Then they killed me! When I woke up, I was surrounded by corpses. My mother, my father, everyone was dead,' he said.

I visited one of these killing fields in 1980. It was near the city of Kompong-Cham between the Mountains of Man and Woman. Some of the mass graves that lay under the scrub bush had been dug open. Rags still stuck to the bones. The skeletons were piled on top of each other. There were broken skulls and scattered bones everywhere. There are times when a reporter's objectivity slips. The image of my Cambodian guide carefully, quietly, leading me through this scene of desolation remains clearly etched in my mind.

In January 1979 the Vietnamese invaded and occupied Cambodia. The Khmer Rouge were ousted and became guerrillas once again. But, for the people, the worst news was that the harvest was poor and hunger stalked the countryside, a harbinger of the starvation that was to plague Cambodia for another ten years. Hundreds of thousands of refugees spilled in every direction, either trying to trek back home or to cross the border into Thailand. The efforts of the ICRC and other relief organizations were thwarted by the parties.

'Every passing day, thousands of children, sick people, adults die in Cambodia for lack of care and food,' said Mr Alexandre Hay, then ICRC chairman.

Meanwhile, those who were still under Khmer Rouge control along the Thai border and in the jungles survived under even harsher conditions. Up to forty per cent of the people who had been herded into the jungle at gunpoint died of starvation or from disease. It was too dark beneath the forest canopy for food to grow, so they had to find it where they could. People were rationed to half a pound of rice a week. Those who finally made it to the refugee camps in Thailand were nothing more than skeletons. The aim of the game seemed to be to control not just the territory but also the people. They were the pawns of war.

'Even in Africa we have never seen anything like this – malaria, kwashiorkor, dysentery, TB ...,' despaired one of the Medecins sans Frontières doctors working at the Mai-Rood camp in Thailand.

'Don't write about this. Nobody would believe you,' Dr Revel said to me in the Sakeo camp. He was sewing up a young girl's stomach wound with a needle

> **❝ When they managed to flee Cambodia, the survivors told gruesome stories. ❞**

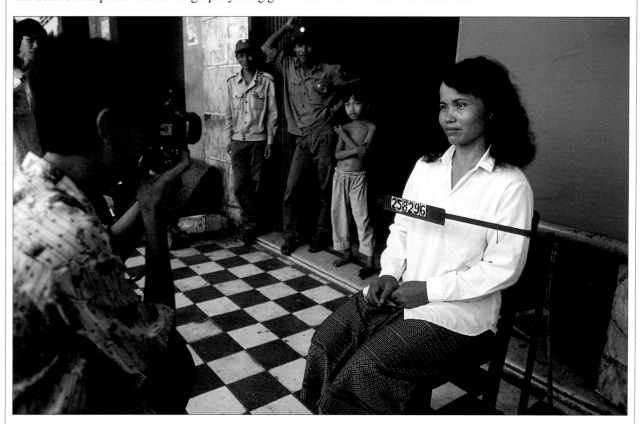

and thread he had borrowed from a visiting journalist. The operating theatre was a tattered tent awash with mud from the monsoon rains.

Many refugees never made it to the relative comfort of the Thai refugee camps because they were turned back at the border. One woman related her experience to me, but refused to give her name. She was in a group of 40,000 dispatched back into Cambodia across steep mountains strewn with landmines. One month later, those who had survived the ordeal trailed back into Thailand. There were only 1,070 in the party.

Life was not easy in the camps. They soon became swollen with hundreds of thousands of refugees. Relief agencies from all over the world, big and small, mounted a massive emergency operation. They collected money; dispatched food, medicine and books; recruited doctors, nurses and teachers; and publicized the Cambodians' plight through the international media.

Operating conditions were extremely difficult. At night, the overcrowded camps fell under the sway of armed gangs of Cambodians who plundered food

ABOVE

Today's identification cards. A pavement photographer takes a picture of a customer for her mandatory government ID card.

RIGHT

The natural pose of a small girl offsets the stylized poster for a beauty salon in Phnom Penh.

supplies and forced young men and women to act as coolies, carrying weapons and rice to the front across the minefields. They threatened to kill anyone who resisted them. Many people were robbed, raped and murdered. This nocturnal mayhem was beyond the aid workers' jurisdiction and there was little they could do to stop it.

As the years rolled by, the violence escalated. Children and women were forced into prostitution. Sometimes their tormentors were the camp wardens. There was extortion and blackmail. A raw violence had been unleashed by a people who had lost all moral values after being brutalized for so many years.

In March 1989, by which time some refugees had been living in camps for a decade, the 180,000 refugees in Site 2 camp became embroiled in the simmering resistance to the Phnom Penh government and the camp became a battlefield. Teenagers were recruited as scouts and porters for the offensive against the government. Rice supplied by relief agencies was collected from each household to feed the fighters. When the offensive failed, the government retaliated by shelling the camp with rockets.

The problem was summed up in a United Nations Border Relief Operation report. 'It is important to recognize that the Khmer political hierarchy of all factions on the border do not distinguish between civilian and military personnel or populations, but view everyone as part of an integrated whole – the resistance,' it said.

For two decades Cambodia had been growing, harvesting and exporting refugees just as it used to grow, harvest and export rice. Entire populations were

RIGHT

The rehabilitation centre for the handicapped in Phnom Penh, commonly known as the Pagoda. Some of the amputees are resident here and make their own artificial limbs. They are helped by Khmer technicians, many of whom are amputees themselves.

BELOW

A homeless man uses his leg as a pillow on a Phnom Penh pavement.

pulverized into dust in the relentless struggle for supremacy. No one will ever know the true mortality rate – one, two, three million slaughtered, starved or left to die without medical care.

Now, as the conflict continues, the majority of casualties are children herding cattle and water buffalo, farmers working in rice paddies, women foraging for firewood. They are victims of the wind mine, a small explosive so light it can float in the wind.

This devastating weapon is central to Khmer Rouge resistance tactics, even though the great majority of those wounded are civilians. If thrown into a rice paddy, it floats just below the surface of the water. Farmers bending over to tend their crops are lacerated on their faces, arms and torsos. Countless boys have lost legs from treading on a mine when they were chasing after their fathers' animals. Mines are also strung on trip wires attached to tree branches. When triggered, they explode at chest height.

What is the cost of all this agony? It will be counted for generations to come. And there is little cause for optimism about the future.

'If you remain on the shore, the tiger will eat you. If you get into the river, the crocodile will have you.' It is an old Cambodian saying.

Patrice de Beer, a Frenchman, is the Far East and Pacific Editor for Le Monde. *As the newspaper's Asia correspondent, he has been witness to Cambodia's upheavals from the fall of Phnom Penh in 1975 to the tyranny of today's refugee camps.*

EL SALVADOR
THE VILLAGE OF FLOWERS
Michael Stuehrenberg

El Salvador's rural peasants have been caught in the crossfire between government forces and the Farabundo Martí Liberation Front for over ten years. Paramilitary units introduced a new device for terror against civilians with death squads. Thousands of El Salvador's rural population have been either murdered or displaced.

ABOVE

A family in the wreckage of their home.

LEFT

Shanty towns are now an inherent part of El Salvador's landscape. For those forced by the army to vacate the countryside, they offer the only affordable alternative to the dreaded refugee camps.

The officer removed his sunglasses with a slow and steady hand and gazed at the crowd that had squeezed into the Plaza Mayor between the barrack gates and the church under a blazing midday sun. The church was an attractive building in the baroque Spanish colonial style with twin towers. It was in no way unusual for that part of the world. But, to a stranger, it looked like the backdrop to a Pancho Villa film.

Many of the audience assembled on the square were *campesinos*, peasants whom the war had driven from their homes in search of protection. They were easily recognizable. Their skin was darker than that of the townsfolk; their smooth black hair not so neatly parted. Little streams of sweat trickled down their tanned cheeks to collect on the collars of their Sunday-best shirts. Not even a gringo could have mistaken them for the rich who, conscious of their expensively imported elegance, sat on the platform in the church's shadow.

The crowds held their breath because they knew the officer was staring into the depths of their hearts. The poor stood clutching their hats, and it now seemed that fear rather than the heat was causing them to sweat.

It was 15 September 1986, the anniversary of El Salvador's Independence Day, and a big occasion for Colonel Navedad de Jesús Cáceres Cabrera. Over a hundred majorettes had passed through the narrow streets of the provincial capital, Chalatenango Ciudad. The regimental band had preceded them. The marching and anthems echoing from the bleached walls of the houses had brought a breath of fiesta to the little town which was otherwise accustomed only to the macabre processions of the dead and wounded.

Colonel Cáceres was a tall, lean man and around forty years old. You could tell he was a disciplinarian by the way he stood. His chest was thrust out so that the decorations on his parade uniform glittered in the sun. He commanded Chalatenango Province in northern El Salvador with a rod of iron. His area saw some of the heaviest fighting between the military and the rebels. Mercy, compassion and indecision were not part of his character, for winning the war had become a personal mission. If victory was finally in sight after six years of fighting, it was thanks to men of Navedad de Jesús Cáceres Cabrera's mould.

'We are winning the war because the people support us,' declared the colonel towards the end of his speech. 'That is crucial. Whoever has the support of the people wins the war.' It was a nice fiesta.

A few kilometres east of Chalatenango Ciudad lay San José de las Flores. The town's name promised flowers, but nothing bloomed for miles around. There was only dust and stones between the dilapidated huts. Scrawny hens scratched in the dirt. Here and there a dog dozed in the sun.

The mood was not festive in San José de las Flores. There was nothing worth celebrating for the 562 people who lived in this village ringed by treeless yellow hills. They had gathered at the church for their own special meeting. It was led by a young priest who had recently arrived from Italy. He said he was a missionary, but many believed he was a martyr.

'We give thanks to God that our eight sisters have been set free from the barracks in Chalatenango Ciudad. But we ask Our Lord to set Colonel Cáceres on the path to enlightenment and Christian compassion,' he intoned softly. 'Amen,' responded the congregation.

The church was nothing more than a stone box. There were crude wooden benches in its musty interior and a table that served as a simple altar. The chapel's improvised, half-complete appearance matched that of the faithful who had turned up in clothes that had been repaired too often. They wore

down-at-heel boots and ancient straw hats that, day by day, shaded but never cooled the coarse brown peasant faces.

The sisters to whom the priest referred stood by the altar. They had returned from the provincial capital that morning, empty handed but alive. The Citizens' Committee had sent them to Chalatenango Ciudad to buy medicine the previous week. They had gone on foot because there was no car in San José de las Flores, and the mules were needed in the fields.

At the first roadblock the soldiers had seized the women and taken them to the barracks. 'You are *masas*,' the commander had yelled, 'and the medicine is for the terrorists.'

The women had feared that something terrible would befall them. However, the Archbishop of San Salvador had managed to contact the Army High Command just in time to secure the women's release. It was a miracle for which the community was now thanking God.

The military's use of the word *masas* was the result of a misunderstanding. The guerrillas belonged to the Farabundo Martí National Liberation Front

ABOVE RIGHT
Young guerrillas pause for a rest in the mountains of Chalatenango Province. They moved in small bands of less than half a dozen. As ephemeral as the wind, the army had failed to subdue them.

which described the people as 'the masses', in Spanish *masas*. The government had concluded from this that they were rebel supporters, hence the frequent civilian massacres and the dreadful reputation of the armed forces.

Officially, the army had suspended their fight against the *masas*. 'So much has changed,' Colonel Cáceres explained to me after his speech at the Plaza Mayor. '*Unidos para reconstruir* has won the people over to our cause. Every day, *campesinos* voluntarily come to the barracks to give us information about the terrorists. The people support the army.'

Unidos para reconstruir, reconstruction through unity, was the name of the operation that was supposed to restore law and order. The objective was to gain the sympathy and support of the people, a key factor for either side in this unconventional war. The campaign was supposed to bring development, with the construction of schools and hospitals. In reality, it was a military sweep of the areas that were heavily infested with guerrillas.

Territorial gains had become irrelevant in the conflict. According to the military's thinking, it did not matter whether Colonel Cáceres's share of the barren hills and arid ravines in Chalatenango was a third or only a quarter. 'All we need to occupy is the six inches of space between the *campesinos*' ears,' explained the colonel. He had embarked on psychological warfare to win over the hearts and the minds of the people.

LEFT

A soldier rests in a ransacked house during a military sweep through a rebel area.

❝ It is very difficult for us to separate the sheep from the goats in the villages. Occasionally the death of innocent people is simply unavoidable. ❞

RIGHT

A bewildered woman with her relative who was wounded in an aerial bombardment by the army on the town of San Pedro Nonualco.

That was the theory. In practice things were a little different. The guerrillas were still in Chalatenango Province, operating in small bands of three or four. They were as ephemeral as the wind, and the army had failed to drive them out.

The army toured the villages to hold forth on the evils of revolution and hand out sweets to the barefoot children. The colonel had issued an edict that every house must be painted white, chiefly to eradicate the slogan 'Viva el FMLN' daubed in red on the dirty walls. But by the next morning the slogans were there again, vivid red on gleaming white.

On the night after the fiesta, the heavy thump of artillery shook me awake in my scruffy hotel room. I could hear the crumping of the guns at irregular intervals as I lay there in the blackness. They could not have been aiming at anything in particular because it was too dark to see. I could tell from the noise that they were shooting in the direction of some villages in the dusty no man's land. According to my map, it was in the direction of San José de las Flores.

‘ We had lost everything, our land,
our homes, members of our family.
Now we were supposed to sit in a
camp waiting for this war to end. ’

Civil war had so traumatized the country that 700,000
displaced people fled the countryside for the safety and
desperation of shanty towns.

The next morning I asked the colonel what all the fuss had been about. 'Nothing,' he said. 'We just release flares so that the terrorists cannot approach town under the cover of darkness.' I asked him who lived in San José de las Flores. 'No one,' he said. 'The town has been abandoned for years. Once in a while the terrorists pass through there.' He forbade me to go there to see for myself. The road to the village was mined, he warned.

The following morning I walked into the village to be met with an effusive welcome. A little girl presented me with a bunch of flowers and the children's choir sang a song. The Citizens' Committee proudly showed me the school they had just built, the crude church and a system of reed pipes that carried water to some of the houses. Their resources did not stretch to providing electricity.

The village I saw was only a few months old. Officially, life had stopped there four years ago when the army had transported all the inhabitants to Chalatenango Ciudad. From there, the Red Cross helped them to get to San Salvador, fifty miles away, where they were put in church camps for displaced people.

In 1986, over half a million out of the five million population were classified as displaced: refugees in their own land. There was no longer a place for them at

Unidos para reconstruir, reconstruction through unity... The campaign was supposed to bring development, with the construction of schools and hospitals. In reality, it was a military sweep of the areas that were heavily infested with guerillas. **,**

liberty so they had been interned. But whereas life on the land was filled with fear, life in the camps was without hope. Many *campesinos* felt the latter was worse than the former.

A young man called José Lisandro Monge voiced the people's anxieties. 'We had lost everything, our land, our homes, members of our family. Now we were supposed to sit in a camp waiting for this war to end. When the end would come and what would follow, no one could say. That's why we decided to act independently.'

José was among the first group to resettle San José de las Flores in early 1986. They soon found themselves cut off from all supplies of medicine and food. Seven children had already died of hunger and disease, the villagers said, and the army's shelling and occasional infantry operations had jeopardized their first harvest of beans and corn.

Despite these hardships, people continued to flock into San José de las Flores. Each one had his own story to tell. I talked to a white-haired woman who sat on a bench in the sun, her hands folded in her lap. From time to time, as she recounted what she had seen, her words tailed off into soft whimpers. I sat and listened, but felt powerless to help her.

'The soldiers locked us all in the church, then fetched the men out one by one. They tortured the boys. They cut a cross in their stomachs with a knife. Six of them died. They said we were all guerrillas.'

LEFT

Families caught in the crossfire between rebel and army troops are left with gutted buildings for a home.

Suddenly an aircraft appeared. It circled above us like a vulture. The men looked about them anxiously. The children and some of the women ran in panic to the edge of the village where they had scraped out trenches as protection against aerial bombardments. Only the old woman sat motionless on her wooden bench.

'It is probably a reconnaissance flight. They are looking for you because they know you have disobeyed the colonel,' said José. He grabbed me and we dodged from hut to hut until we reached some eucalyptus trees. I stood there, feeling vulnerable and exposed. When the plane finally disappeared over the horizon, I decided to take my leave of the villagers. They had enough problems without having to shelter me as well.

Two days later I was thrown into a cell, the guest of the Policía de Hacienda, who deal with political offenders. Not far from the village I had run straight into an army patrol. They had taken me to San Salvador under heavy guard.

They had confiscated all the tapes I was carrying at the time of my arrest. If anyone played them back, they would hear the villagers relating their woes, which included atrocities carried out by the army. But I was not concerned

about this. I had warned everyone to be careful not to mention their name or anyone else's when talking into the tape recorder.

My gaolers were friendly enough. But there were tell-tale signs of sinister goings-on. My sleep was disrupted by a pistol being fired outside the cell door. In the duty officer's room I saw a prisoner with his arms bound behind his back. Blood was dripping from his lip down his chin and on to a soiled T-shirt. He had an ugly wound above his cheek. I asked the officer if the man was a *masas*. He looked baffled. 'No,' he said, 'he's a terrorist.'

Even the political police found it difficult to distinguish between a *masas* and a terrorist. My interrogator, an intelligent young man called Ramón, explained that the line drawn between guerrillas and sympathizers was becoming increasingly blurred. 'The people take part in elections and then they collaborate with the guerrillas,' he said.

ABOVE

Neighbours come to look at the bodies of five women, including a mother and her two young daughters. Two of the women were pregnant. They had been tortured and shot, then dumped at the cemetery of Apopa at 11.00 a.m. the previous day. No relatives had come to claim them for fear of being murdered as well.

'This makes every *campesino* outside our zone of control a potential *masas*. It is very difficult for us to separate the sheep from the goats in the villages. Occasionally the death of innocent people is simply unavoidable,' he told me.

I cast my mind back to the old woman in San José de las Flores. Was she aware of her guilt?

After three days in the cells, the duty officer sent for me. He said my activities had endangered national security. I was to be deported.

A few weeks later, an Amnesty International official came to see me at my office. 'I'm afraid I have bad news for you,' he said. My heart filled with dread.

After my departure from San José de las Flores, Colonel Cáceres had swept into the village with a detail of 500 men. The soldiers had encircled the school and dragged the teachers out. Then they went into the classroom and told the children they wanted to play a game with them. They were going to play some tapes to them and the children had to guess who was speaking. Afterwards, they took several of the villagers away with them.

I was horrified by what had happened – the seduction of the children, the unwitting betrayal of the parents. My newspaper stood by me and persuaded the West German Ministry of Foreign Affairs to lodge a protest with the government. In El Salvador the Archbishop of San Salvador lobbied on our behalf too. We did everything we could to save the people who had been taken

ABOVE

Army check-points to scrutinize travellers' identities and carry out body searches are frequent.

RIGHT

A girl stands in rain and mist at the grave of a relative.

prisoner. Eventually, our efforts paid off and they were set free. You can imagine my relief.

Over the years, there has been no fundamental change in the *masas'* situation. Just recently I heard that some of the peasants from San José de las Flores had been arrested while buying provisions in Chalatenango Ciudad. They had been unable to prove their innocence because, as long as the war is still on, anyone finding himself in the wrong place at the wrong time is guilty.

Maybe the old woman who sat on the bench in the sun could explain why the persecution and the deaths continue. But I am not sure she is still alive.

Michael Stuehrenberg, a German, left Agence France Presse to work full time as a war correspondent in Latin America and Africa. He contributes to Die Zeit, Geo *and other publications.*

❛ As long as the war is still on, anyone finding himself in the wrong place at the wrong time is guilty. ❜

LEBANON
BRIDGING THE DIVIDE
Fiammetta Rocco

ABOVE

The waterfront of the Christian seaport city of Jounieh.

LEFT

Relatives of bombing victims in west Beirut identify the corpses.

The civil war that has been raging in Lebanon for fifteen years has degenerated into fratricidal strife. Somehow commerce manages to survive despite the ebb and flow of Beirut's residents who flee the city whenever shelling intensifies.

We were well into the coffee before I asked to see the gold. My host for dinner that first evening in Muslim-controlled west Beirut was Edmond Naim, Governor of the Central Bank of Lebanon: a bull-headed, balding man, with sharp black eyes that sometimes smiled. I had heard that he kept 300 tons of gold in the basement. It had survived fifteen years of war, partition and occupation in one of the world's most lawless cities. And I wanted to know if it was still there.

Dr Naim prepared the minty cucumbers himself; for security reasons, he said. There were black olives from the Bekaa Valley, and thick golden hummus, which we scooped up with bread. We ate on the terrace of his tiny flat atop the central bank building. Half a mile away was the notorious Green Line, a no man's land seven miles long that snakes through the city, dividing it into east and west; Christian and Muslim. Had we been able to see out of the flat across the street we would have noticed that every window of the prime minister's office was broken. But twelve-foot walls rose up around us, and all we could see of the sky above was a tiny square in which shone the hungry full moon. It was like sitting in a drawing room without a roof. The walls were supposed to keep out the shellfire that came sporadically from the Christian side of the Green Line, even in ceasefire. I don't know how well they worked.

Before I raised the subject of the gold, Dr Naim told me how he came to have a wall-to-wall lawn on his roof-top terrace. 'I tried many things,' he said. 'And then, you know, one day I discovered Astroturf. Only Astroturf doesn't shrink or wrinkle or fade.' In a city where death comes so fast and so unexpectedly, durability is a matter of pride among Beirutis.

Naim wiggled his slippered feet into the prickly green evenness. He is seventy-two now, a former law professor who knew little about banking when he was first offered the post in 1985, at an age when he could have retired. He didn't. Though a Christian, Naim lives in and works in Muslim-controlled west Beirut because that is where the bank is. He has often been threatened. And ever since his friend Rashid Karami, the former Prime Minister, was blown up by a bomb under his seat in the ministerial helicopter in mid-1987, Dr Naim has never left the building; never crossed the concrete esplanade with its bullet holes the size of grapefruit, to bid a friend goodbye or to go out for a drink.

In short, he is immured in his office on the wrong side of a divided city, guarding Lebanon's gold for Muslim and Christian alike. His German wife, Hedda, lives in the family home in east Beirut. She gardens, cares for the animals and watches over Naim's collection of law books, the biggest law library in the Middle East. Once a fortnight, she crosses the Green Line to bring him frozen dinners, fourteen at a time. In the tiny galley kitchen where he prepares our dinner hangs a framed copy of Rudyard Kipling's poem, *If*. The last line is, 'You'll be a man, my son.'

For over a thousand days, Naim has lived like this. Inside the bank, he is safe from kidnap and assassination. His refusal to abandon the post has touched the ordinary Lebanese deeply. He is the guardian of their wealth; the gold, they believe in their darkest moments, is proof that their nation is still solvent. To outsiders it makes him seem impartial, safe, aloof from the everyday politics of Lebanon. Anyone who wants to see Naim has to visit him in the bank, as Elias Khazen, the Interior Minister, found to his cost last January.

Khazen, a Christian, had taken refuge in the Summerland Hotel in Muslim-controlled west Beirut when fighting between two Christian factions made the east particularly dangerous. It was the first time that Christian ministers had left the relative safety of their eastern enclave for the Muslim quarter, and Khazen believed it was up to Naim, who was junior in rank, to visit him. Not the other way round.

When Naim refused to leave the bank, the minister sent a government police force to arrest him. Naim's bodyguards opened fire when four policemen burst into his office, and sealed all the exits from the bank before trapping the four in the basement, not far from the gold. Khazen was forced for a while to quit the government, but Naim never left the safety of his guardhouse.

Naim is a brave man because he works for other people in a country where self-interest is the normal creed of survival. But there's a price to be paid for being brave in that way, and Naim knows he needs his frozen dinners, his Astroturf lawn, in short the mundane aspects of life, to keep him in touch with the ordinary people. They are the ones he is being brave for.

As I sat on his terrace, I wondered what was at the root of Naim's power. In a nation of such consummate traders, it had to have something to do with the gold hoard in his basement.

Had the governor actually seen it?

'Every month.' He spoke slowly. He said it was because his false teeth didn't fit as they should, and the dentist hadn't been in to visit him.

'What does it look like?'

'It is kept in a vault, in special boxes.'

'Can I see it?'

'There are many keys and many people involved.'

'Perhaps when the governor pays his next monthly visit?'

'Perhaps,' he said, fiddling with the offending dentures. 'Perhaps.'

As I walked back to my hotel, my escort, Daoud, who was also Naim's driver, asked me the question that seemed to possess everyone I met in Lebanon, 'The gold. Have you seen it?'

Later that night, I lay awake doing sums in my head while the moon shone, wavy and white, through the windows of my room. Across the street, an empty cinema housed hundreds of homeless refugees, lined sleeping on the floor where the seats should have been. The bank's annual report listed its assets as 312 tons of gold: about ten million ounces. The hoard amounted to two-thirds of Lebanon's gold reserves, and was worth four billion US dollars on the open market. The remaining third was in Fort Knox. Why not keep it all there?

❛ Naim is a brave man because he works for other people in a country where self-interest is the normal creed of survival. ❜

Storm clouds create a chiaroscuro landscape in the
Kadisha Valley.

ABOVE

The aftermath of the September 1982 massacre of Palestinians in the Shatilla and Sabra Camps. Over a thousand Palestinian refugees were slaughtered by Phalangist forces. Here women search for their husbands and sons amongst the bullet-riddled corpses.

LEFT

The survivor of a heavy artillery attack on one of the Palestinian camps.

I had heard there were two keys to the strongroom, one kept in east Beirut and the other in the Muslim west and that the gold was stored in wooden cases with ancient, thick red seals. It had not been unpacked since it had arrived in Beirut from Constantinople after the collapse of the Ottoman Empire in 1918.

Ten million ounces, 400 ounce bars, packed perhaps eighty to a box. That meant over 300 boxes, a stack the size of a double-decker bus. Why didn't someone carry it off? Why did they trust him not to sell it? Was it really there?

It is not only the gold which gives Naim his lustre. From behind a barricade of salmon-tinted sandbags in his sixth-floor office, he runs Lebanon's finances, welding order out of economic despair. Stubborn, old-fashioned and arrogant, he has a fine tenor voice and can be charming. Selim al-Hoss, Lebanon's Muslim Prime Minister, considers him one of his great Christian friends. On the other hand, a former Finance Minister, Elias Saba, who is a Christian, calls Naim 'a pain in the ass'.

Largely because of his strenuous efforts to keep Lebanon's economy from completely breaking down, however, business still goes on as surely as the gunshots and the shelling. Workers and farmers go about their labour, contracts are signed and, whenever the shelling stops, Beirut boutiques pull out the latest European fashions.

But Naim is more than a central banker. The vacuum in Lebanon's political leadership means that he often has to operate without orders from the top, weaving a treacherous course through the back, and sometimes blind, alleys of local political factions, for whom bloodshed is as habitual as the drinking of arak. In effect, with Lebanon's statehood virtually collapsed into civil strife, the central bank governor has become the symbol of everything that still works in that tattered country.

He may not go out to work, but he knows nonetheless the effect of what he does. In September 1988, after the Lebanese Parliament failed to elect a successor to the outgoing President, Amin Gemayel, Naim turned to a visiting banker and said, 'The real government of Lebanon will be here, in my office.'

Palm Sunday in the Christian village of Kafachima on the outskirts of Beirut.

Amal Shiite militia in the shell of a bombed-out building overlooking Christian positions in Beirut.

❛ The walls were supposed to keep out the shellfire that came sporadically from the Christian side of the Green Line, even in ceasefire. I don't know how well they worked. ❜

' For a six-month period in 1989
the shelling was so heavy in Beirut
that it emptied the city of nine-
tenths of its population. '

The aftermath of the Quarantina massacre. A young boy
strums a mandolin looted from a burnt house. Lying in a
puddle in the foreground is the body of a young girl.

That Naim was successful in keeping a vestige of normal life going in Lebanon while it remained leaderless for well over a year in 1988–89 is largely due to two things: the gold in his basement, and a pig-headed sense of fairness. He pays civil servants' salaries, including those of the divided Lebanese Army. His trucks deliver cash to banks on both sides of the Green Line, he formulates economic policy, and his bank funds the national debt. In short, he controls the purse strings of the nation. What he refuses to pay for are imports of arms, or personal favours. When General Michel Aoun, the then Maronite leader, demanded a pay rise for his soldiers in 1989, Naim refused on the grounds that either all soldiers, Muslim and Christian, were paid extra, or none at all. Aoun never got his money.

The man who said no to Michel Aoun is a Maronite Christian who grew up in the Chouf Mountains, the stronghold of the Druse Muslims, a proud and hardy people. The independence of mind that drove Naim to refuse Aoun's request for money has made him a hero to some Christians and many Muslims, who draw comfort from the fact that he has fallen out at one time or another with every religious faction in Lebanon, and will, therefore, favour no one.

For a six-month period in 1989 the shelling was so heavy in Beirut that it emptied the city of nine-tenths of its population. With the help of his four vice-governors, who are drawn from the three main Muslim groups and the Orthodox Christians, Naim kept Lebanon working by taking over the responsibilities of other government departments that couldn't function – for example, the power company, Électricité du Liban.

One of Beirut's most peculiar sights is that of thousands of small wires trailing from the pylons on Beirut's main streets. In Beirut, the power company won't hook you up to the mains, so you help yourself, any way you can. The people who attach these lines are power poachers, and don't pay their bills. So Électricité du Liban turns to the central bank for funds to pay for fuel imports.

Nor do most Lebanese pay taxes. So the government too turns to the central bank for funding. The bank, in turn, using its gold as collateral, finances itself by asking commercial banks to deposit some of their money in its coffers. For this, the bank pays them interest of sixty per cent a year, sometimes more.

Another of Naim's main tasks is to keep these banks supplied with cash. Once a month, a single truck emerges from the underground car park at the central bank, and meets up at the gate in Rue Masraf Loubnane with a military escort drawn from the Syrian army. The truck is loaded with Lebanese banknotes, packed in bags and ready to be delivered to banks around the city. When it delivers to east Beirut, an escort of Christian Lebanese Army soldiers takes over from the Syrians at the Green Line.

Each banknote bears Naim's signature, and it is he who orders them from the British security printers, De La Rue. In 1989, twenty million US dollars in new Lebanese pounds were crated up in De La Rue's warehouse on their way to Beirut when General Aoun fired the opening salvo of his Liberation War. With Beirut airport closed, Naim had to choose between flying the banknotes to Cyprus, and then transferring them by boat to Jounieh, the Christian port north of Beirut, or flying them to Damascus and bringing them into west Beirut by road through Syrian lines. He chose neither, and the notes stayed in the warehouse until a ceasefire was signed six months later, in October 1989.

Even when his own building was being shelled, Naim stayed at his post. Of the 500 staff at the bank, twenty per cent or so live in east Beirut and cross the Green Line every day. During that time, most stayed at home, and the bank was run by a devoted skeleton staff, many of whom bunked down in sleeping bags in the waiting-room outside Naim's sixth-floor office when the shelling proved too dangerous for them to go home. Late at night, Naim would retire

upstairs to his little flat, and call his wife in the east. Often they talked about Ülingen, the village in Germany where they plan to be buried.

Before leaving Lebanon, I visited Naim one last time on his roof-top terrace. A week earlier, some of Lebanon's parliamentary deputies had gathered at a disused airbase in the north of the country to elect a president. At the time, it seemed a gesture of hope: one that would become all too futile when he was assassinated ten days later. The new president was decapitated by a car bomb that blew him up on the way to his inauguration. On the morning I visited Naim, another car bomb had gone off, next to a playground off Rue Hamra. Four children were killed. As stretcher bearers hacked away the charred and twisted metal to get at their tiny bodies, I noticed, out of the corner of my eye, a dwarf. He was climbing on top of a pile of garbage on the pavement in order to reach the windscreen wipers of a car parked alongside. He was trying to issue a parking ticket. Years of crushing devaluation had reduced the value of the fine demanded to about 25p. Counting the stairs to Naim's apartment, I wondered how many paid up.

Dr Naim knew I was leaving more confused than when I had arrived, and that I would ask again, as I had done on every visit, to see the gold. I had heard many stories: it was there, it wasn't, it had been divided up, put away for safekeeping – in the Chouf Mountains, in Syria, in Washington. What I hadn't encountered was a single person who had ever looked into that vault.

As I climbed up through the damp smell of concrete (they were finally fixing up the shell holes), I realized that it didn't matter whether I saw it or not, whether it existed or not. In Beirut it was enough for people to believe it was there. Lebanon has a troubled soul, but ordinary people are happy to believe in ordinary things: a lawn that doesn't shrink or fade, a parking ticket if you misbehave and something in the bank.

Fiammetta Rocco, a Kenyan, read Arabic at Oxford University and works for the Independent on Sunday *in London. She spent three weeks with Dr Naim in 1989.*

RIGHT
While they rounded up Palestinian men and boys for execution in Quarantina, the Christian Phalange fighters allowed the old to escape to west Beirut.

BELOW
Patients in a Beirut hospital. The windows have been sandbagged against artillery shelling.

AFGHANISTAN
THE SEEDS OF SORROW
Bernard Dupaigne

In 1978 the mujaheddin rose up against the central government, prompting a Soviet invasion the following year. The losers in this conflict were the farmers and herders whose families, homes and animals were killed and destroyed by bombs and landmines. Afghanistan's refugee population of 5.5 million is the largest in the world.

ABOVE

Mujaheddin greet each other with an embrace.

LEFT

In Bamian, the heart of Afghanistan, stands one of the greatest art treasures of the world : a 200-foot statue of Buddha carved from the rocks by monks in the seventh century.

had heard nothing, but my horse reared violently. I was flat on my back on the ground before I understood what was happening. I saw a giant cloud of dust rise from the steppes. Two bombs had been dropped over the mud-brick village.

I had been about to ford the river downstream from a party of women who were enveloped in multi-coloured veils. They had run away from the fighting and been waiting with their children for the caravan of camels that had been sent from the village to fetch them.

The camels were caught mid-stream when it happened. They had scattered in panic when they heard the loud crump of the explosions, splashing clumsily through the water. Now they stood with their headropes dangling, growling with displeasure.

It was 1983, and the country was in a state of turmoil. We had been walking all night, retreating from the tanks that were the vanguard of bitter fighting that had raged for three days. When the plane screamed low over our heads, I presumed that it was returning to base and that we were safe. I was dreadfully wrong. It released its last bomb above the ford where the women squatted. The noise was deafening and the shock of the explosion flattened me to the ground. Clods of earth rained down on me. My terrified horse bolted with the stirrups beating wildly against its sides.

Chaos ensued. Everyone was crying with pain or terror as a result of the carnage. People ran in all directions. The ground was littered with the dozens of sheep and cows that had been killed by the flying shrapnel. Lying next to me was a young child with her face partially blown away. She was as limp as a rag doll, and as silent.

A young shepherd boy about fifteen years old ran past wailing and clutching his shattered, blood-soaked shoulder. I had nothing to give the wounded that could either save them or ease their last moments of agony. There were only the few tranquillizers I had in my pocket. I handed them to the boy's father, knowing they would not forestall the inevitable. The boy would almost certainly die from infection within a few days.

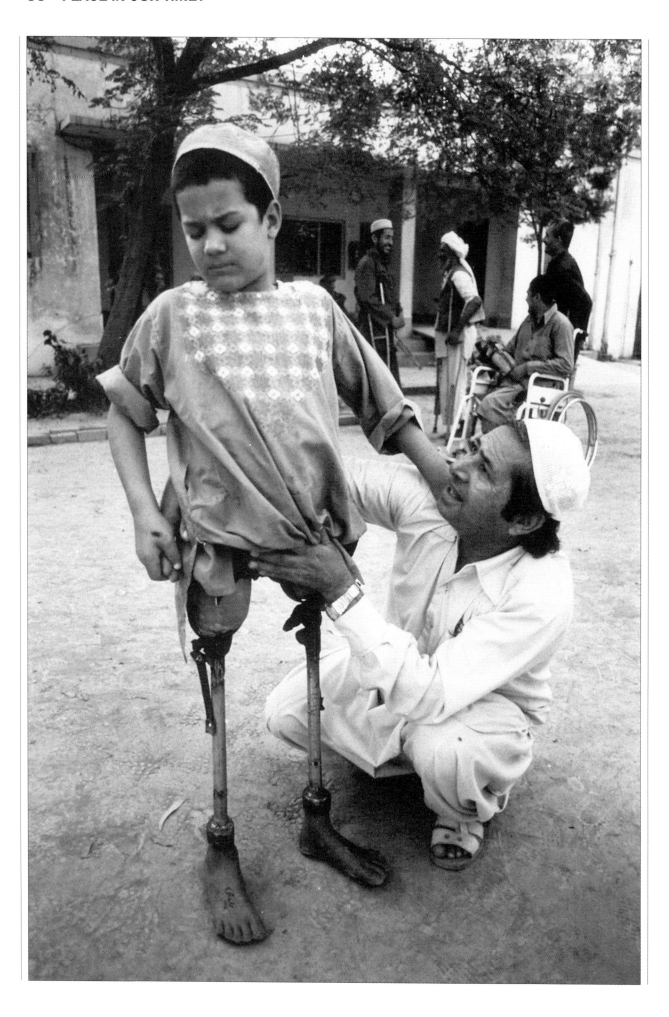

Many crippled children, such as twelve-year-old Abdulh Ali, have been treated at the International Committee of the Red Cross Centre at Peshawar in Pakistan. He lost his legs on a landmine.

❛ The ground was littered with the dozens of sheep and cows that had been killed by the flying shrapnel. Lying next to me was a young child with her face partially blown away. She was as limp as a rag doll, and as silent. ❜

A boy shop assistant in Bird Street in Kabul.

Across the river all was desolation. Men were frantically digging shallow graves to bury the dead before continuing their flight. The plane had been guided by a reconnaissance helicopter and the pilot had scored a direct hit on his target. The bombs had demolished the house of the local warlord, a respected cleric. He had been holding a meeting when it happened. I had slept in the house three days before. Now Maolawi Abdul Hakim and his twelve companions lay buried in the rubble.

The third bomb seemed to have been dropped on these helpless civilians almost as an afterthought. The pilot had released his first two bombs with skilful precision only a few instants previously. What could he have been thinking of when he dropped this one?

'You are leaving, but we have to stay behind,' said one of my companions on this precipitous journey. 'There are going to be reprisals now with tanks and helicopters. The tanks have only to move up the Murghab river valley to destroy our villages. We can't stop them with our small arms.'

The man who found my horse was a local villager called Mohammed Hassan. One day he had been to Herat, a large town 125 miles to the west, to sell the carpets his family made. He was picked up by the military and sent to an army base in the north. After a month, he managed to escape with four Kalashnikov AK47 assault rifles and a mine-detector. It was the custom for deserters to report to the first resistance committee they came across. They were supposed to deliver any weapons they had. In return, the commander gave them some money to enable them to return home.

Another man I knew was captured while he was threshing his wheat. The soldiers burnt his harvest and put him into solitary confinement for sixteen days. He was eventually sent to Herat to guard a cement factory. He managed to escape during the second month there. His friend had tried to run away a few days before and had been shot dead. Desertions were so frequent that the army buried small anti-personnel mines around the perimeters of the garrisons.

Later, on that same journey, I was travelling with a party of Afghan men along a stream. My horse skidded on the slippery pebbles and fell. 'What's the

RIGHT

A refugee gets his hair trimmed by a street barber in Peshawar.

BELOW

A man displays one of the anti-personnel mines that are dropped around villages from helicopters.

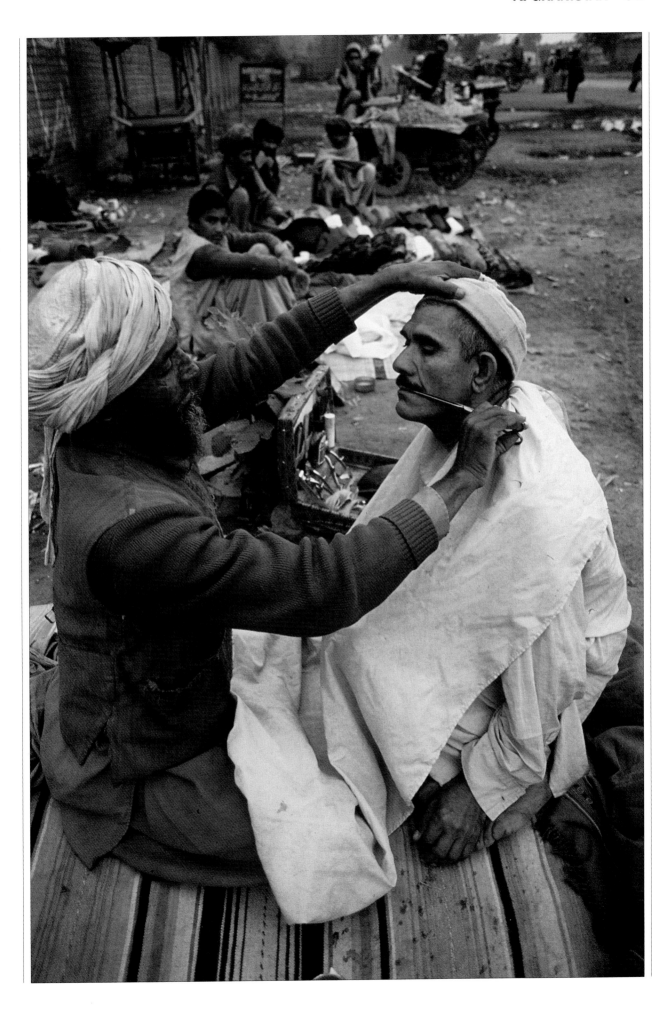

matter? Come on, whip your horse. It's dangerous around here!' urged my companions. Like other foreign journalists and doctors and like my friends, who had been imprisoned, tortured and press-ganged into the army, should I be injured I could not seek medical treatment in a town in case I was gaoled.

We met a group of about fifty young men on foot, carrying knapsacks and wearing broken shoes. They had staves as protection against the wolves which sometimes attacked travellers. They were going to Iran to look for work as labourers, ditch-diggers or chicken farmers. They said they would be gone for six months, perhaps even a year or two. Poor harvests had emptied the country-side as people desperately sought a means to support their families.

The situation had deteriorated that year. Two consecutive droughts had been followed by a cold snap. Swarms of grasshoppers had denuded the hill-sides of northern Afghanistan and the remaining wheat was diseased. Pesticides had disappeared since the war. The country was on the verge of famine.

My companions' casual banter stopped and they were silent. We were passing through Saour, one of countless ghost villages. It had been surrounded by tanks, helicopters and infantry and virtually razed to the ground. The 500 houses were empty shells, their mud walls vitrified by the heat of the fire that had raged through the village. Entire families had died here.

It was 1990, seven years later. The previous year there had been frequent ambushes along lonely routes and, inevitably, as the trip wore on, so the tension mounted. Reconnaissance trips were made by experienced guides mounted on racing camels before anyone dared venture forth. Despite these precautions, refugees returning from Pakistan laden with provisions travelled only at night.

We were meandering through the desert. Our vehicle seemed to float, transported on an ocean of sand. It was tempting to abandon the rutted tracks but, if we did, there was a very real danger of getting stuck. A rocky spur, ravaged by winds, pointed the way. The setting sun threw shadows into the crevices of the hills. In a hollow that had managed to retain a little rain water, a shadow rose. Friend or foe?

The wraithlike apparition in front of us was a shepherd, wrapped in a huge, rigid felt cape that served as home and shelter, protection against the raging heat and the cold of approaching nightfall. There were less than twenty sheep left to herd, the remains of his magnificent flock of 300 head. War had decim-ated all the flocks.

The cunning of the caravan leaders and the shepherds had been useless against the marauding helicopters that suddenly appeared out of nowhere to reconnoitre the timeworn tracks. They would drop out of the sky and let off bursts of sub-machine gunfire. By destroying the herds, they destroyed the economy of the country. Sometimes the helicopters landed and manhandled a few sheep into their holds. Fresh meat was a welcome change for soldiers far from home who were tired of eating Russian or Bulgarian tinned food.

I was travelling with a relief worker who was a specialist in hydraulics. Between us we hoped to repair some of the irrigation systems in one of the districts of Kandahar Province. We wanted to reconstruct what madness had destroyed. If we succeeded, the farmers would be able to sow their wheat, and the vines, which had shrivelled up from lack of water, could be brought back to life. Some of the fields were already green·thanks to our work the previous year and the tenacity of the Afghan peasants who were determined to rebuild their devastated villages.

For these people, water was the wellspring of life. With its return, the houses could be repaired and the harvest brought in, making it possible to bring home the families that had been left in camps in neighbouring Pakistan for as long as eight years. When the aerial bombardments began, about eighty per cent of the people fled. Afghans form the largest refugee population in the world.

ABOVE

There were no essential commodities such as matches and diesel oil in the countryside. Men and boys never went on shopping expeditions for fear of being inducted into the army. But for those who lived in the towns, the entrepreneurial spirit flourished. Here veiled women are offering a second-hand radio for sale.

RIGHT

Wounded mujaheddin and refugees at sunset prayer at an International Committee of the Red Cross hospital near Peshawar in Pakistan. In front are relatives who often serve as attendants to the patients or as hospital workers.

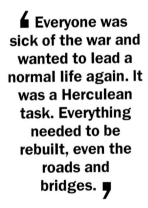

' Everyone was
sick of the war and
wanted to lead a
normal life again. It
was a Herculean
task. Everything
needed to be
rebuilt, even the
roads and
bridges. '

The village where we were heading was completely camouflaged from the air.
Its pre-war predecessor had been abandoned. The once beautiful mosque, with
its ornately-carved wooden panels, was in ruins. The mihrab, the prayer niche
indicating the direction of Mecca, had crumbled to dust. Ten years ago, the men
met here on Fridays for a morning of prayer which invariably evolved into a
discussion of village affairs. Now they attended a new mosque that had been
carved into a cliff face. It had a minute courtyard that was open to the sky.

For the past five years the village had led a subterranean, secret life. Without
subterfuge, nothing survived on these flat, dry plains where even the tiniest red
handkerchief was visible from the air. The houses were buried in the ground
and their courtyard walls covered in branches.

From above, it was impossible to detect any sign of life. People no longer
lived outside, but stayed in the comparative safety of their homes. Once a day
the women drew water from the river. The men visited their old fields from time

Mujaheddin pray five times a day when most lay aside
their guns, but some prefer to keep them slung over
their shoulders.

ABOVE
A mujaheddin greets goats that in due course will be slaughtered and eaten.

to time to do some maintenance work, to give the vines a little irrigation water, when there was any, to prevent them from drying out.

The roof of the guesthouse where we stayed reached just above ground level. It was made of compacted earth on reed supports. Whenever anyone walked over our heads, we were showered with earth.

I knocked at the door of Juma Khan, a local leader. He opened it a crack and, when he realized who we were, bid us enter. Juma smiled and looked embarrassed. 'Please forgive me. I cannot receive you properly. I have hardly anything left.' Tea and other commodities sold in shops were a rarity. No one in the countryside owned anything that was machine-made or imported, such as oil for lamps, radio batteries, soap, cloth, matches or sugar.

As I made a tour of the village, I was surprised to be surrounded by laughing children. They all wanted to have their pictures taken with their friends. Young boys with eyes outlined in kohl and little girls tried to wheedle me into taking a snapshot. But they were disappointed. My camera was not the kind that produces an instant photograph.

The windows of their underground schoolroom were slits at the top of the walls. The children sat in the gloom and practised Arabic script in their exercise books. The schoolmaster gave me a warm welcome. The school had been financed by our humanitarian organization.

There was a single class for all ages, containing about fifteen boys and five girls. They were being taught writing, reading, mathematics, history, geography and religious instruction.

It was a poor school, but the children were nevertheless privileged. The government had not paid the salaries of the rural schoolteachers for ten years. A whole generation of schoolchildren had been sacrificed to the war.

At first, conditions were so difficult that schooling was ignored. Gradually, the resistance administration realized an attempt had to be made to educate the young people. With local resources and help from abroad, numerous little schools were established, employing former schoolteachers or religious scholars who could at least teach reading and writing.

The following day, I set off to deliver a diesel-powered corn mill to a district at the foothills of the mountains. Diesel was very hard to obtain because it was one of the strategic goods that the government-held towns refused to issue to the rebellious countryside. Yet wheat had to be ground into flour as bread was the basic foodstuff. Isolated from the monetary economy, villages had been forced into self-sufficiency. Wheat, grapes, fruit, the occasional egg and a little meat from the family flock were the only resources.

I convened a meeting with the village elders. The topic was an important one – how to clear the irrigation channels that used to bring water to 200 houses. It

❝ Isolated from the monetary economy, villages had been forced into self-sufficiency. Wheat, grapes, fruit, the occasional egg and a little meat from the family flock were the only resources. ❞

was decided that the owners of the fields which would be irrigated would come
and work with the local farm labourers on this job.

Everywhere on the plain, as soon as an irrigation ditch was serviceable again,
there were people ploughing. Plough oxen were rare as most had been butch-
ered by gunfire, besides, a pair of oxen, which only do two months' ploughing, are
expensive to maintain for the rest of the year. A few landowners had been able to
buy a tractor which they hired out to their neighbours.

Everyone was sick of the war and wanted to lead a normal life again. It was a
Herculean task. Everything needed to be rebuilt, even the roads and bridges.

RIGHT

An official uses a stick to beat
back women and children
fighting their way into a UNICEF
supply centre at a village
twelve miles from Kabul.

But many had faith in the future. I could tell because they had begun to plant young vines in their yards. It was a long-term investment – a good sign.

Bernard Dupaigne, a Frenchman, is an anthropologist at the Musée de l'Homme (Museum of Mankind) in Paris. He has been working in Afghanistan for nearly twenty years, to begin with as an anthropologist and then as a relief worker and agricultural expert. His book, Le Guide de l'Afghanistan *(Afghanistan Guide) was published in 1989.*

The chaos of trying to secure a place on a truck destined for the comparative safety of the bush country is far preferable to the turmoil these Liberians want to leave behind.

LIBERIA
THE CARNIVAL COMES TO TOWN
Mary Anne Fitzgerald

An old and incapacitated woman in a wheelbarrow joins the exodus from Monrovia. By October 1990, the tenth month of the civil war, over half a million Liberians had become refugees in neighbouring countries.

Liberia is one of two black African countries never to have been colonized. The other is Ethiopia.
A bloody tribal civil war that began in January 1990 has resulted in the deaths of thousands of Liberian civilians.

Monrovia is a funky town. It straddles mangrove swamps on the western shoulder of Africa, just above the armpit. Much of it is very African, of course. Women stride through the mud balancing plates of fish on their heads, and dogs scrounge for scraps from rotting heaps of garbage. People jostle at the bus depot for passage into the interior. The rickety wooden stalls that sell cigarettes, drinks and food add to the roadside chaos. The scent of frangipani wafts over bungalows that look on to the grey breakers of the Atlantic Ocean. Flies gather on anything that is edible.

Those who have been there say the yellow taxis and ducks dabbling in the open drains remind them of Haiti. Perhaps it is the air of abandon and decay that strikes the familiar note. Half a block from the downtown business section, there are moss-encrusted houses raised off the ground on concrete blocks or, sometimes, just boulders. The sloping tin roofs frame windows where men and women sit and watch the world go by. Across the street, young boys stand under a storm drain to get a free shower from a tropical downpour.

There is also the imprint of another culture, another epoch that has been distorted by distance and time. Liberia was founded in 1847 by slaves freed from the cotton plantations of the American South. Just as Peter Stuyvesant stole Manhattan from the Indians, so these black families bought the land on which they built the capital. The knockdown price accepted by the local people was 300 US dollars, with some beads and cooking pots thrown in.

The settlers then began exploiting the native Liberians with a ruthlessness that far outstripped that of their former American masters. They created an elitist political dynasty of Americo-Liberians which ruled uninterrupted for 143 years. The native Liberians were referred to as aborigines and left to their own devices, except when they were enslaved and exported to other countries in the region, a practice which continued well into this century.

The political dynasty came to an abrupt and bloody end in 1980 when Samuel Doe, a young master sergeant who had not had time to finish high school, and a member of the Krahn tribe, executed a successful coup. The power shifted, but the American legacy endured.

A fifteen-mile drive through gleaming green vegetation leads to Clay Ashland, a residential centre that has some fine examples of plantation-style houses, even though wood rot has long set in to their porticoed façades. The men who live there wear chinos, sneakers and alligator shirts. Their wives attend church every Sunday morning wearing tiny hats with tiny veils à la Jackie Kennedy in the late 1950s.

Back in town the street stalls display packets of Marlboro and Wrigleys chewing gum. There is Kraft salad dressing on sale in the supermarkets. A man in a baseball cap sits on a stool outside the Pacific Video Store. Set back from the road is the Rooster Sudden Food Restaurant.

Guests at the Holiday Inn can watch addicts lounging in the crack dens across the road. The police wear the cast-off summer uniforms of the New York Police Department – their navy blue shirts still have the NYPD insignia sewn on to the shoulder. But that was in the days when a modicum of law and order still held sway over the jumble of tin shacks, churches, office buildings and concrete block houses.

If Monrovia is a pastiche of *Gone with the Wind* and Papa Doc, painted on to an African canvas, then it has created an ethos that is unique. The faded gentility and religious devotion are counterbalanced by another darker side of the national psyche that pays fealty to sorcery.

Leopard men are supposed to stalk villages in the bush. A diplomat told me he went out deep-sea fishing and drifted on to a corpse bound to a crucifix and painted with voodoo signs. Monrovia may be funky, but even when there was peace, a disquieting undercurrent ran beneath the bustle of its daily affairs.

When I arrived in June 1990, the sinister atmosphere was tangible. For the past five months, rebels from Gio and Mano tribes had been oozing through the countryside like a mudslide. Now they were only a few miles beyond the city perimeter. Everyone was tense and jittery. There were soldiers everywhere, manning roadblocks, riding in the backs of pickups with their guns sticking up like antennae.

The men who had unleashed this civil war were so bizarrely dressed that, at times, they seemed more like a carnival parade than a guerrilla army. They marched into battle in bathrobes, women's dresses, underwater goggles and wigs pillaged from the houses of expatriates living on the Firestone rubber estate. Comical as these trappings were, they masked a brutality that was far from laughable. They were armed with a hodgepodge of automatic weapons, stiletto knives and machetes. The carnage inflicted by this makeshift arsenal was lethal. Journalists travelling with the rebels reported seeing skulls stuck on pikes and the corpses of Krahn soldiers, partially devoured by scavenging dogs.

Tens of thousands of Gio and Mano who had been in the path of the fighting had swarmed into the city, believing its tin shacks and shoebox houses would offer safety. But, as the net drew tighter, there were tales of nocturnal witch hunts by armed men in uniform. They raided homes in the middle of the night, pulling out Gio and Mano men and shooting them.

My first stop after landing at the downtown airport was the John F. Kennedy Memorial Hospital morgue. Standing in the stench-filled heat of the corridor, I watched the bloated bodies of three of the city's elders being wrapped in polythene. A couple of ears were missing and some chunks of flesh had been hacked out, probably with axes.

'Make it snappy,' said a sweating mortuary attendant as he sealed down the sheets with Scotch tape. 'We gotta get out of here before nightfall. You can take photos, but don't show our faces.'

The murders had shocked and frightened the community and gave rise to weeping and wailing at the outdoor funeral held the next day beneath a mango tree in Clay Ashland. The following Sunday, in the Providence Baptist Church

❝ The situation got worse every day, every week. All the refugees were looking for safe places to sleep. ❞

‘ The men who had unleashed this
civil war were so bizarrely dressed
that, at times, they seemed more like
a carnival parade than a guerrilla army. **’**

Many rebels wore gruesome masks and clothes pillaged
from people's homes which created a carnival-like
atmosphere amidst the senseless killing.

on Ashmun Street, the congregation sang 'Come Ye Disconsolate' and silently joined hands while Reverend Momolue Diggs prayed for an end to the bloodshed. 'We can't do this alone Jesus. We call on you to give us strength,' he cried.

It was a situation that called for the assistance of humanitarian organizations and they were there – the International Committee of the Red Cross, Belgium's Medecins sans Frontières and the Catholic Relief Services. I left Monrovia the afternoon of that passionately moving church service, on the last evacuation flight out to safety. The aid workers stayed behind.

As the weeks went by, I wondered how they were and worried. The rebel advance into town had cut off not only the water and electricity supplies, but also the telephone link to the outside world. They and the Liberians they had gone to help were isolated in a ghetto of horror. They had no protection.

I followed the events that unfolded by listening to the BBC and reading copy from the wire services. When, in due course, the massacre occurred, I cried. For those of us who had been there, the denouement was as inevitable as a Greek tragedy, but it was an atrocity that shook my faith in humanity. What, I wondered, could anyone have done to save the lives of those hundreds who had been killed?

As the summer wore on, I flew to Berne to talk to Peter Lutolf who had been in charge of the ICRC operation in Liberia. Then I took the train westwards to Ostend and visited Reginald Moreels, chairman of the Belgian Medecins sans Frontières. He too had been in Monrovia, operating on both sides of the front line. Thus I was able to piece together a picture of what had happened.

Lutolf's seventeenth-century flat was crammed with mementos from his postings around the world. Delicate porcelain bowls from Cambodia were stacked on the floor. The walls were lined with books from floor to ceiling. He was convalescing from a bout of cerebral malaria. Even so, he looked ten years younger than when I had last seen him.

He placed a pair of long-stemmed glasses on the coffee table and uncorked a light red wine from Germany he wanted to try out. We toasted each other and he began his story.

'The authorities didn't trust us because they thought we would interfere in their internal affairs. As soon as the conflict started in Nimba county and the presence of the ICRC became a fact, the government began to retreat from negotiations with us. The more the rebellion got out of hand, the more the ICRC was considered to support the rebels.

'Wherever we are working we are in favour of the victims of such a conflict. There were a lot of innocent victims amongst the Mano and Gio. We had to help them. The government was against all these people and gave them a hard time. Of course, you could understand the government's attitude. In their eyes, we were prolonging the conflict. But if the Krahns had been the victims we would have supported them impartially.

'It was very difficult to know how many displaced Gios and Manos came looking for relatives in Monrovia. Maybe 50,000. Maybe 70,000. People came to our office to ask for news. We were able to trace some of them.

'The army saw them as potential rebels who would be ready to fight them if the conflict spread to Monrovia. So they did horrible things. The Krahns attacked Gios and Manos and killed them before they were killed themselves. They raped the girls and cut the men into pieces and threw them on the beach. It was terrible. They created a psychological terror.'

I asked if there was anything he could do to stop it. 'This is a basic problem for the ICRC and all humanitarian organizations. During the eleven years I have been with the ICRC, I have noticed a deterioration of political and humanitarian behaviour in the countries where I've worked. You can't do anything if governments are not willing to respect basic rules. I can't go to the

minister of defence and say, "If you don't stop these atrocities, you'll be brought to court and punished." It's all based on respect for humanitarian principles. It's really difficult.

'The situation got worse every day, every week. All the refugees were looking for safe places to sleep. Some of them began coming to St Peter's Lutheran Church. Then it was like a fire. The first night there were about two to three hundred people. They had no food. Only a few personal belongings. They just entered the compound. No one could stop them. The second night there were perhaps a thousand. The third night three thousand. After two or three nights, there were about five or six thousand people fearing for their lives who just poured in. In one week there were about seven places – churches, missions and a school – looking after them. The church leaders came to us and asked us to protect them. We were in a real dilemma. We knew the army had a close eye on these places. We had to do our best to protect them, but we were creating a situation that would make them an obvious target for the army.'

I had visited St Peter's Lutheran Church when about 4,000 people were jammed into the one-acre compound. There were six toilets. The pastor was worried about an outbreak of cholera.

But it was the spectre of death that worried the people who were there. The compound was enclosed by shoulder-height brick walls and a rickety metal gate that was chained shut at nightfall. Flying from the four corners were the Red Cross flags. Whenever a truckload of soldiers drove past, a frisson of apprehension rippled through the crowd. They knew the walls could be easily scaled and the Geneva Convention meant little.

Ivan Quown had a typical story to tell. He was the only survivor after the army had shelled his village with rocket-propelled grenades a few weeks before. I asked if he felt safe. 'We are in God's hands,' he said.

The previous month, government troops had stormed another Gio and Mano refuge at the United Nations headquarters. They abducted and killed thirty men. As a direct result of this, the United Nations closed its offices and evacuated its staff.

In mid-July the army looted the hotel where Lutolf was staying. He moved out and camped in the ICRC offices. Soon that also became too dangerous. The ICRC team was receiving constant death threats from soldiers who accused them of being rebel supporters.

By this time, two different rebel factions were conducting sporadic firefights with the army all over town. Lutolf and his colleagues moved into a United States embassy flat that had been vacated by its occupants.

It was virtually impossible to cross town. The front line shifted from block to block and you never knew who might shoot you. With law and order in abeyance, the blood lust had risen in the gorge of every man who held a gun. The shops had closed long ago and people were starving to death. They were shot if they looted. They were shot if they belonged to the wrong tribe.

An Englishman saved his gardener from summary execution by buying him back from the soldiers for twenty-five US dollars and a packet of Marlboro. Another prisoner was not so lucky. 'We've got to shoot someone,' the soldier said, casually putting his gun to the man's head and pulling the trigger.

Although it became literally impossible for the ICRC to visit the compounds, they received reports from a Ghanaian businessman called Leroy who regularly slipped across the lines to visit Lutolf. 'I have seen so many things. I don't fear for my life any more. I know that I could be killed, but at least I can do my best to bring you news,' he told Lutolf.

Meanwhile the Medecins sans Frontières (MSF) team were working at St Joseph's Catholic Hospital, the only hospital still functioning. Every day they drove out to pick up the wounded off the streets. Once they came across six feet strewn over the road. The bodies were lying in the bushes nearby.

The hospital was still under government control when Reginald Moreels received an SOS from Omega Base. Some 20,000 people had sought refuge at this United States communications installation which was behind rebel lines. Many of them were wounded and urgently needed medical attention. Moreels managed to negotiate safe passage with the army and the rebels to visit Omega and the MSF team set off in two cars filled with medical supplies.

BELOW

Just as in medieval times, the besieged capital suffered severe food shortages. With the spectre of famine looming large, malnutrition rapidly rose to eighty per cent. Residents faced the choice of starving to death or running the risk of being shot as looters. These terrified boys, accused of stealing, were lucky to have escaped with a beating from a rebel fighter.

'We arrived at a military camp and had to wait an hour to discuss things. Then the commander said, "No problem. You can go on. You will be preceded by a tank." We didn't want that because we would get shot at. At last they let us go. We were travelling down the main road to Guinea which was the front line. There was no one on it. We got the rebels on the radio and they said, "Okay. Okay. We can see you. Come on. We are waiting for you."

'We went another hundred metres. The first shot. We braked immediately. We dropped down. There were two men including the other surgeon in the car behind. They had stopped as well. We got up and looked slowly around, but we couldn't see anyone. So we went on another fifty metres and there was another shot that hit the car. The shots were coming from quite far away but we could hear the clack of the bullets against the bodywork of the car. Then five or six soldiers appeared out of the bush. They were drunk and drugged and had hateful eyes.

❝ When a non-governmental organization that respects neutrality has absolutely no protection at all, it's madness. We have worked in lots of difficult situations in different countries, but there it was impossible. It was the most dangerous place that we have ever worked in. ❞

BELOW

Rebel leader Prince Johnson remonstrates with one of his own men having just shot him for allegedly profiteering from the sale of rice. The dying man said, 'Why me?' and died seconds after this picture was taken. He is handcuffed to Jacques Montouroy of the Catholic Relief Services, who was released the following day. The men were distributing rice when the tragic misunderstanding occurred. The dead man had borrowed a bib from the Liberian Red Cross to indicate that he was performing humanitarian work.

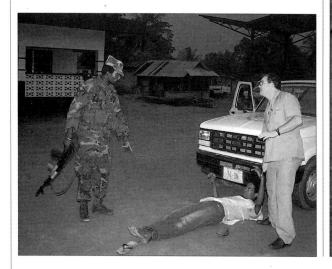

'We decided to turn round. When a non-governmental organization that respects neutrality has absolutely no protection at all, it's madness. We have worked in lots of difficult situations in different countries, but there it was impossible. It was the most dangerous place that we have ever worked in.'

By late July the fighting was so heavy that the MSF team were trapped inside the hospital. There was a constant flow of wounded into the wards. Sometimes they had to stop work and lie on the floor to avoid the bullets.

Then one night, at 2.00 a.m., about thirty soldiers climbed over the walls of the St Peter's Lutheran Church compound. When they finally left, they had bludgeoned, knifed and shot about 500 people to death. There were bodies sprawled on the altar and under the pews. Women had had their skulls smashed in by rifle butts. Their babies were left alive, still tied to their mothers' backs. Some of the babies had had their hands hacked off.

The MSF learned about the massacre the following morning when over 100 wounded turned up at the hospital. About 600 were wounded in all. Moreels had by this time returned to Belgium, but he knew the story well.

❝ **For those of us who had been there, the denouement was as inevitable as a Greek tragedy, but it was an atrocity that shook my faith in humanity.** ❞

ABOVE

A victim of the rebel takeover of Paynesville, a Monrovia suburb, lies in a sodden, deserted street. Corpses such as this, many of them months old, litter the city as there is no one to remove them and nowhere to take them.

'They had cut throats and stab wounds in the stomach and bullet wounds and hands cut off. It was five days' work. The first day the medical team treated the worst wounds. The second day they treated the bone injuries. They tried to go to the church but they couldn't get there. Some of the patients were brought in cars by the army.'

That same day, Leroy walked to the United States embassy compound to tell Lutolf of the massacre, but the ICRC team could not reach the church either.

I asked Lutolf how he felt about it all. He leant forward, resting his elbows on his knees, and looked at the carpet. 'It is more than sad. You cannot understand all this brutality. You cannot explain it, but you see it, you hear it, you feel it.'

Liberia is an extremely strange country.

Mary Anne Fitzgerald's story is based on interviews with officials working for the Red Cross and Medecins sans Frontières in Monrovia and on information she gathered on a visit to Liberia in June 1990.

Campesinos prepare a traditional potato meal in their hut. Guinea-pigs kept under the bed provide a cheap and nourishing supply of meat.

ABOVE
Life in the Andes has changed little since the Spanish conquistadores arrived five centuries ago.

PERU
A MARCH OF DESPAIR
Alfonso Centeno

For the past twenty years terror has been a way of life in Peru where the Sendero Luminoso (Shining Path) battle against government forces. Over 20,000 people have been killed, most of them of indigenous Indian stock. Another 10,000 have disappeared without trace.

Breathing is difficult at an altitude so high it is half-way to heaven. However, riding a mule at 12,000 feet along a narrow and precipitous track is even more arduous. There is a bottle of rum to ward off the icy wind but, as for my mount's surefootedness, there is only blind faith. The occasional bird flutters overhead. Patches of yellow grass cling to the rocks.

Life is rugged here. The people who live in the Andes have sought shelter in its ravines and valleys, cocooned by centuries-old tradition. Isolated by geography and their language, Quechua, they have few links with the modern world. In this bitter climate, there is only one crop a year of potatoes and maize. The luckier ones have small herds of llamas, goats and sheep. On the whole, property is communal, just as it was five centuries ago at the time of the Incas. This is a culture of poverty.

Women are washing clothes in the river where the track curves to approach Chunchumaka village. Our greeting is met with silence as they stand with hands easing stiff backs, staring at some distant point where the snow-capped mountains touch a porcelain-thin sky. My guide explains in Quechua that I am a journalist, that we have come as friends. Their taciturn answer needs no interpretation. The appearance of a stranger is a cause for concern in this tightly-knit community, where unheralded arrivals have spelt tragedy.

During nine days in April 1990, an army patrol carried out a punitive expedition against the people of the Apurímac and Cusco districts of the South Andes in Chumbivilcas Province. As they passed through the villages, they enacted a sinister charade of the road to Calvary, dragging villagers behind their horses as they rode. New prisoners took the place of those murdered along the way.

By the time the soldiers finally left, thirteen people were dead. Another eight had disappeared. That is the number counted by grieving families and the number in the report written by Friné Peña, Cusco's member of parliament.

The soldiers were looking for members of Sendero Luminoso (The Shining Path), an anti-government terrorist movement that has exacted its own grisly toll from the villages. But it was the innocent peasants, not the guerrillas, who were tortured and killed.

‘ Other men's ideals have created
a chain of ghost villages where
homes have been robbed of their
souls. ’

A barefoot herder with her charge. Llamas, goats
and sheep are usually communally owned, an old
Inca tradition.

Yes, the slaughter was terrible, but it is not the only massacre in Peru's ten-year 'Dirty War'. Retribution in the form of random killing is at the heart of the military's strategy to subdue subversion. After all, said a general, every peasant is a suspected *senderista*.

Terror is not the sole domain of the army. For could it not also be true that every peasant is a government collaborator? The Sendero Luminoso's atrocities can be counted in hundreds. They choose their victims indiscriminately. There are the landowners and those who hold power, but there are also peasant farmers and schoolteachers. There are policemen and soldiers too, but they are only peasants in uniform.

Over 20,000 have died in this undeclared civil war. Most of the casualties were these peaceable people of the Andes, trapped in the crossfire.

Other men's ideals have created a chain of ghost villages where homes have been robbed of their souls. Women and children, widows and orphans, wander aimlessly in the shadow of dilapidated churches. The traditions and religious festivals that kept their culture in focus have ebbed into emptiness. Everything dies under the weight of this war which the poor have neither caused nor been able to comprehend.

Several weeks before I travelled to Chumbivilcas, I met José C. in Lima. He was thirty but looked at least a dozen years older. He was slow to talk, because misplaced trust is laden with consequences. 'I, Sir, am married and have four children. Where are they now? I had potatoes and a few sheep. I have nothing now. This year it was my turn to host the village festivities. There will be no fiesta now. That's for sure. First the Sendero Luminoso fighters, then the soldiers, stole everything.

'The [Pentecostal] Church brothers helped me to come to Lima. I have no friends here. I had to run away because I was told that the lieutenant Negro was furiously looking for me. He accused me of spreading lies. I have said nothing, Sir. Here I work as a gardener's assistant and I am also a servant. I take messages, mow the lawn, walk the dog. There are a few girls who cook and do the cleaning, but they never speak. I got this job because the head gardener is an

LEFT & RIGHT

Rural lifestyles are as rugged as they were when Spanish conquistadores subdued the Incas five centuries ago. The legacy of that ancient and splendid civilization has been poverty and hardship.

BELOW

Retrieving garbage from dumps that can be recycled is one way of eking out a living.

evangelist. He has told the bosses that I am a cousin of his. They will accuse me of being a terrorist if they find out that I am from Apurímac. The bosses are very rich. I have never seen them. I think that they are gringos.'

José C. works in a mansion in the Planicie district of Lima. There is a swimming pool, a tennis court and 5,000 square metres of garden. There are four domestic staff, excluding José. The bosses are not gringos, but an ancient and wealthy Lima family. For them, the travails of José's family are far removed.

José is one of a host of peasants whom violence has turned into a refugee. The process of adaptation to city life is difficult. Most end up in the overcrowded slums of the coastal towns. Some make a subsistence living by either begging or selling car spares, sweets and cakes on the streets. José, like many of the young girls, was lucky. He found work as a domestic servant.

It was only after much persuasion that he agreed to recount the events that took place at Huacullo. 'I, Sir, am an evangelist, and God would not allow me to lie. There were twenty-five soldiers on horseback under the command of a lieutenant whose men called him Negro.

'They entered the village of Huacullo, in the province of Antabamba in Apurímac on the afternoon of 20 April. Most of the soldiers spoke in Quechua, but a Quechua from a different region. I saw them making themselves comfortable in the village school.

'They were very alert. They had brought five detainees with them. There was also an eight-year-old girl whom they had dragged in. Next, they ordered us to get out of our houses and assemble in the main square.

'Once there, they arrested seven of us peasants and locked us up in one of the school classrooms. The detainees they had brought with them were put into another room. We were forbidden even to look at each other.

'The next morning, the lieutenant left the village on patrol while a group of soldiers stayed behind. They were quite drunk by noon. Then it all started. They kicked the seven of us mercilessly until blood came out of our eyes. For hours they wanted us to confess, but we had nothing to confess. They said that the peasants had met the Sendero Luminoso fighters twice. "You are fellow fighters," they said. We even offered them money to leave us alone.

'Víctor Huachaca Gómez explained to them that we were evangelists and that we had not met with the Sendero Luminoso fighters. It was all to no avail. He died that very same day from torture.

‘ On the whole, property is communal, just as it was five centuries ago at the time of the Incas. This is a culture of poverty. ’

'Early the next morning, before the lieutenant returned, we were set free. Then the whole patrol departed. We, the people of Huacullo, watched them disappear over the horizon. We thanked God for that.'

Two days later, the lieutenant called Negro led his column of soldiers up to the mean huts of the village of Pomallacta. The same six prisoners straggled behind them. It was rumoured the little girl had been taken hostage because the soldiers could not find her father.

Negro and his men spent the night there. They ordered two sheep to be slaughtered and cooked for them. Then they raped the women who had prepared the meal, and tortured the husbands.

This is what Marcos H., who was at Pomallacta, had to say. 'The following day they took Eustaquio Sainoa, Jesús Jauja Suyo and me, with them. We were about eight prisoners. There was also a silent and confused girl. On the road we met eight people from Ccassahui looking for a donkey. However, the soldiers did not believe them and thought they were terrorists, so they were arrested and taken with us.

'We were escorted to Soracocha pool. It was 5.00 p.m. They made the people from Ccassahui take their clothes off. They pushed their heads under the water and kept them there so they couldn't breathe. They kicked them and beat them with their rifle butts. They wanted them to confess to their ties with the Sendero Luminoso. In the end, some of them admitted their guilt without knowing what they were confessing to.

'When dusk fell, we arrived at a house that belonged to an old couple. The inhabitants of the nearby houses had run away when they saw the patrol coming. We spent the night there with the soldiers and the girl. This poor girl said nothing. She could do no more than stare.

'That very night I managed to untie my feet and escaped over a hill which was covered with cacti. I came under heavy fire, but I got away all the same. Hours later, I met my wife at the entrance to my village. At first she thought I was a ghost. It wasn't easy to convince her that I was not.'

After an arduous trek, I arrived at the village of Ccassahui on a Sunday. My guide and I were accompanied by a schoolteacher from Santo Tómas. His gentle manner elicited the villagers' trust. Without him their silence would have been impenetrable. It was a feast day, and the women's dark serge dresses were decorated with sunbursts of bright ribbon. They offered passers-by grain, tubers, skeins of wool, fruit, dried meat and tiny salted fish. The men bartered

for scrawny sheep and small long-haired horses. They were drinking a home brew distilled from sugar-cane that gave a boisterous edge to their bargaining.

The elders had gathered at the community centre to discuss weighty matters. There was the case of the young man accused of petty thievery. There was also a decision to be reached as to whether or not the irrigation ditch should be widened. They greeted us effusively with the traditional offering of a glass of local rum followed by coca leaves slaked with lime.

They were loquacious and relaxed, recounting some of the lengthy stories that made up their tapestry of oral history. It was difficult to turn the chat towards the punitive expedition. The introduction of tragedy on such a happy day would not show respect, the schoolteacher warned.

I kept quiet, biding my time. My patience was rewarded much later when a man from the nearby village of Ccollpa pulled me away from the revellers, indicating that he wanted to talk. His tale sent a chill of horror down my spine.

He, too, had seen the column of soldiers, the prisoners and the mute girl. One had been poisoned and died. Four had been set free. The rest were taken to Ocapallullo Hill. It was 27 April. They were tied up and made to stand in a row against the side of the hill. The soldiers laid a charge of dynamite at their feet and lit the fuse. Then they unleashed a hail of bullets into the explosion. The corpses were stuffed into crevices in the rock and covered with straw.

ABOVE

Young boys sleep on the streets in Lima. Nearly 20,000 civilians have been caught in the crossfire between soldiers and guerrillas.

LEFT

A porter carrying his load to the market at Puno. Refugees from the fighting end up in slums in the coastal towns. Many are beggars and street vendors. Others become prostitutes and domestic servants.

'Sir, I only want justice to prevail,' said the granddaughter of Hermenegildo Jauja, one of those who were killed. 'My grandad was all I had left. My father was taken away by the Sendero Luminoso the year before last and my mother died of smallpox.'

For many, one sorrow overlaps the next, saturating them with despair. But the villagers of Ccassahui were determined to seek redress for the atrocities the soldiers had committed. On 28 April they arrived in the provincial capital of Santo Tómas to put their case before Judge Mario Castilla. At first they were ignored, but their persistence wore him down and he agreed to visit their village.

Assent was not given lightly, however. Even the due process of the law exacts its tribute. The judge wanted horses provided for himself and his police escort.

A horse is more valuable than a car in the roadless mountainsides of the Andes, but three days later the villagers walked into town leading mounts for the judicial party. The judge scoffed at their offering and said the animals were not enough. He would need at least thirty. The villagers nodded mutely. They knew the demand was preposterous, but were determined to meet it. They sacrificed what little goods and money they had to hire even more horses. And still the judge did not go to Ccassahui to exhume the peasants' bodies, even though an inquest was required by law.

But the villagers were not to be deterred. The brutal murders of their neighbours and families were an issue freighted with responsibility. They were fighting for the honour of the dead. At last they obtained permission to exhume the corpses. It took a whole day to strap the bodies on to mules and carry them back to Santo Tómas. The victims were given a proper burial after a post

> **❛ For many, one sorrow overlaps the next, saturating them with despair. ❜**

ABOVE

A woman displays the ID card of her daughter who was murdered two years previously.

LEFT

A child of Indian stock finds a safe ride on his mother's back on market day.

mortem had been carried out. Nevertheless, no charges of murder were brought against anyone. No one was brought to trial to avenge the atrocities. Instead, the story of the unjust judge, the horses and the post mortems was buried in a voluminous affidavit compiled by their member of parliament, Friné Peña.

There is a postscript to this tale of shattered lives. On 29 April the military patrol passed through Huacullo on its way back to the garrison in Antabamba. They now had another four detainees. But the silent girl was not one of them.

Alfonso Centeno is a pseuodynm for one of Peru's leading journalists. His name has been withheld so that he can tell the truth about what is happening in his country.

ACKNOWLEDGEMENTS

The publishers would like to thank John Easterby of Magnum Photos Limited for his assistance in helping to produce this book.

ASSOCIATED PRESS
Alistair Sinclair 112

Carol Beckwith & Angela Fisher 10 *top & bottom*, 14, 15

Julio Etchart 58

FRANK SPOONER PICTURES
Karim Daher 102 *top*, 106–7, 109, 111; James Hamilton 18 *top*, 19

James Hamilton 18 *bottom*, 22, 23

MAGNUM PHOTOS LTD
Abbas 37, 41, 83, 89, 93 *top*, 99, 118; Micha Bar'Am 77; Ian Berry 36 *bottom*, 122; Cornell Capa 64–5; Raymond Depardon 96–7; Stuart Franklin 100–1; Jean Gaumy 69; Thomas Höpker 126; Sergio Larrain 114 *top*, 119; Peter Marlow 30, 31, 36 *top*; Don McCullin 73, 76, 80–1; Steve McCurry 46, 47, 50 *top & bottom*, 51, 54, 55, 88, 91, 93 *bottom*, 94, 95 & cover; Susan Meiselas 59, 66; Inge Morath 74–5; James Nachtwey 26 *bottom*, 34–5, 39 *top & bottom*, 63, 87, 90, 98; Gilles Peress 70 *bottom*; Eli Reed 70 *top*, 82; Marc Riboud 42, 43, 86; Sebastiao Salgado 12 *top & bottom*, 13, 17, 20, 21 *top & bottom*, 25, 44–5, 48, 49, 52, 53, 56, 57; Ferdinando Scianna 16; Chris Steele-Perkins 28–9, 32, 38, 40, 60, 61, 62, 67, 68, 78, 78–9, 84–5, 87, 114 *bottom*, 116–17, 120, 121 *top & bottom*, 124, 125; Alex Webb 127

POPPERFOTO/AFP
Pascal Cugot 113; Joël Robine 105

ROBERT HARDING
David Lomax 26 *top*

SYGMA
A. Balaguer 123; P. Robert 102 *bottom*, 110